RATHAD IARAINN NAN EILEAN

A TRAVELLERS & TOURISTS GUIDE TO THE WEST HIGHLAND LINES

MICHAEL PEARSON

WAYZGOOSE

www.wayzgoose@jmpearson.co.uk Tel: 01283 713674 Copyright: Michael Pearson. All Rights Reserved First edition 2001 - ISBN 0 907864 87 2

One Man's West Highland

Michael Pearson unravels the West Highland Lines' rich history

WHEN the rock star hero of Scottish novelist Iain Banks's Espedair Street elects to escape from the pressures of stardom and go in search of the love of his life, it's to Glasgow's Queen Street station that he takes himself, boarding a steam-heated train of elderly carriages "damply warm and enveloping" which fill him with "an odd mixture of longing and contentment." He was treading a well-worn path. Generations of sassenachs have found solace and stimulus on a West Highland train. Some made it just as far as the steamer pier at Arrochar, others reached Loch Lomond and The Trossachs. Generally you needed time and money to stretch further, to follow the Iron Road to the Isles, to Lochaber, infinity and beyond. My Uncle George used to go boy-scouting in Ardlui, resourcefully heaving his kit out of the window of the slow-moving train, to avoid a long walk back to the campsite with a tent and a collection of billycans on his back.

IT is no exaggeration - well not much of one - if I tell you that the West Highland Railway we know (and love!) today owes its very existence to one Victorian gentleman's frustration that the post and the daily newspapers didn't arrive in Fort William until early evening; sometimes, if the weather was more than usually bad, until the next day. It seemed particularly galling to this Mr Boyd (for that was the name of our hero) that a one-horse-town like Kingussie - then the railhead for the Lochaber district, fifty miles away - should have its post and its papers (courtesy of the Highland Railway) in the morning when a town the size of Fort William didn't. Mulling on such matters, he rallied the support of local landowners who, like him, had been disappointed that an earlier attempt to attach Fort William and Lochaber to the railway network had come to nothing. These gentlemen contacted the Caledonian Railway to see if they'd

like to build them a railway - preferably a direct line from Glasgow. The Caledonian demurred, but their second approach, to the equally redoubtable North British, received a favourable reply.

THE North British had been this way before. They'd been behind the Glasgow & North Western proposal of 1880. In those days Scotland's north-west was widely recognised as one of the most backward regions of Europe. A speculative consortium of mostly English financiers planned a line to run northwards from Glasgow via Milngavie and along the east bank of Loch Lomond to Crianlarich from where it would head for Fort William by way of Glen Coe and thence, with a causeway along Loch Ness, to Inverness. The scheme, not surprisingly, met bitter opposition from entrenched interests: other railway companies (notably the Highland Railway who had hitherto managed to keep Inverness to themselves) steamer operators on both Loch Lomond and the western seaboard and, perhaps most redoubtable and reactionary of all, lairds and landowners, who wanted the West Highlands unchanged and unsullied for themselves and their deer. A Parliamentary hearing concerning the project lasted two months. The scheme's barrister stressed the imbalance which existed between Scotland's east coast fishing ports, where some four hundred miles of seaboard were served by more than forty railheads, compared to the west coast, where the figures were twelve-hundred and two respectively. The railway's opponents countered that west coast fish didn't taste as good as east coast fish and that therefore little would be gained from speeding up their transport. Then the arguments for and against turned to sheep, the Glasgow & North Western claiming that there were almost half a million sheep north of the Great

Glen dying to be transported by train, whilst the Highland Railway claimed half that figure, insinuating that what animals there were would be better catered for by themselves.

IN retrospect it seems ridiculous that so much time and effort was expended, though one can well imagine a repeat performance were some new railway proposed to cross the Highlands now, after all, see how long it took for Britain to come to terms with the need for a high speed link to the Channel Tunnel. After two months it took the committee just five minutes to reject the railway. How differently the social and economic history of the west coast of Scotland might have developed, and what a railway it would have been; one hundred and sixty seven miles of scintillating scenery if nothing else.

MR Boyd and his backers lodged a bill with Parliament to build their West Highland Railway in 1889. It differed from the Glasgow & North Western in that it was planned to leave the existing North British network at Craigendoran, near Helensburgh on the Clyde estuary, and find its way up the west bank of Loch Lomond. A similar route was suggested through

Crianlarich to Bridge of Orchy but then, rather than go directly through the mountainous country of Glencoe, the new proposal would cross Rannoch Moor (in a distant echo of a Thomas Telford road scheme) and approach Fort William from the east via Glen Spean. Perhaps most significantly, there was no hint in the new proposal of setting out to reach Inverness. Thus the Highland Railway had no real case for objecting to the new line, whilst the Caledonian, who claimed (probably with some degree of truth) that Fort William could be much more easily linked to the railway network with a coastwise line from Connel Ferry via Ballachulish, could not argue that the new West Highland proposal would not provide Fort William and the Lochaber locality with the most expedient route to Glasgow.

THEY partied hard in Fort William the night the news came through that their railway was to be built, though five years were to pass before the first train steamed out, Glasgow bound, on 7th August 1894. The West Highland was no easy railway to build. Five thousand navvies dynamited their way through straths and glens and over moorland wastes and rocky passes. Built to a tight budget, the line's engineers, Formans & McCall, devised a route which would avoid expensive structures such as bridges and tunnels unless there was absolutely no alternative. Incredibly, given the mountainous terrain, they needed to bore only one tunnel (and that of only 47 yards) all the way from Craigendoran to Fort William. But, inevitably, there was no shortage of steep gradients, long hard slogs to the summits at Glen Douglas, County March, Gortan and Corrour. In due course the operating department had to come to terms with the challenging conditions, mostly by dint of double-heading, for the line's weight restrictions precluded the use of the most powerful locomotives available. It still does - well past their sell-by date Class 37 diesels being retained to haul the Caledonian Sleeper in the absence of any lightweight alternatives with a train-heating supply facility.

THE Fort may have been getting its newspapers in good time, but the west coast's fish merchants were still without rail access along the difficult and much indented shorelines between Strome Ferry and Oban. The original concept of extending the West Highland to Roshven on the Moidart peninsular was blocked by the intransigence of a Professor of Mathematics at Glasgow University who owned sixty thousand acres in the neighbourhood, and to whom the thought of a fishing harbour and a railhead on his doorstep was "abominable". A colleague added evidence that Roshven was difficult to sail into, a statement somewhat at odds with the Admiralty charts which seemed to suggest that it was potentially the best natural harbour on the western seaboard.

AS an alternative, Mallaig Bay, forty miles from Fort William, was chosen as the site for a new port and railway terminus. It would be another difficult railway to construct. Expensive too, and the West Highland wanted the Government to support the project financially. There were precedents for this in Ireland, but on mainland Britain the railway system had been developed by private enterprise. Getting politicians involved only served to delay the project. Ironically, given recent railway history, the Tories were in favour of transport subsidy whilst the Liberals were not. The

---

EDINBURGH, GLASGOW, CRAIGENDORAN, FORT WILLIAM, and MALLAIG.—N.B.

Down. — Week Days.

King's Cross Station, London (St. Pancras), Edinburgh (Wav.), Glasgow (Queen St. L.L.), Glasgow (Queen St. H.L.), Cowlairs, Dumbarton, Greenock (Steamer), Craigendoran, Helensburgh (Upper), Row, Shandon, Garelochhead, Whistlefield, Arrochar & Tarbet, Ardlui for Head of Loch Lomond, Crianlarich 860, 861, Tyndrum, Bridge of Orchy, Rannoch, Tulloch for Loch Laggan, Roy Bridge, Spean Bridge, Fort William, Banavie, Corpach, Lochailside, Glenfinnan for Loch Shiel, Lochailort, Arisaig, Morar, Mallaig.

Up.

Mallaig, Morar, Arisaig, Lochailort, Glenfinnan for Loch Shiel, Lochailside, Corpach, Banavie, Fort William, Spean Bridge, Roy Bridge, Tulloch for Loch Laggan, Rannoch, Bridge of Orchy, Tyndrum, Crianlarich 860, 861, Ardlui for Head of Loch Lomond, Arrochar & Tarbet, Whistlefield, Garelochhead, Shandon, Row, Helensburgh (Upper), Craigendoran, Greenock (Steamer), Dumbarton, Maryhill, Cowlairs, Glasgow (Queen St. L.L.), Edinburgh (Wav.), London (King's Cross).

NOTES.
a Midnight.
c Except Saturday and Sunday nights.
... at 1 46 aft.

FORT-AUGUSTUS and SPEAN BRIDGE.—Invergarry and Fort-Augustus.—North British.

Fort-Augustus, Aberchalder, Invergarry, Invergloy Platform, Gairlochy, Spean Bridge.

Spean Bridge, Gairlochy, Invergloy Platform, Invergarry, Aberchalder, Fort-Augustus.

NRM

LNER WESTERN HIGHLANDS LMS
IT'S QUICKER BY RAIL
FULL INFORMATION FROM L·N·E·R AND LMS OFFICES AND AGENCIES

project became something of a political pawn and it took two years for the Bill for the West Highland Extension to pass through Parliament. Uniquely, shareholders in the line were guaranteed 3% on their capital and a grant of two-thirds was made towards construction of the harbour at Mallaig. Much to the chagrin of other railway operators, preferential rating was given to the new line as well, meaning that it paid only a fraction of its rateable value. The famous McAlpine company were the contractors and much use was made of concrete, a comparatively new medium at the time.

OBAN had got its railway in 1880, fourteen years before Fort William, twenty before Mallaig. Even so it had been a long time coming, the bill for its construction having been presented to Parliament in 1865 and passed in the same year. Ostensibly the seventy mile, east-west route belonged to the independent Callander & Oban Railway, but it was manifestly a subsidiary of that arch rival of the North British, the mighty Caledonian. Two routes crossed at Crianlarich, and though a connecting spur was laid, quite typically it wasn't used - other than by the occasional cattle train - until after the railways were Nationalised in 1948.

DIFFICULTY in attracting financial support delayed construction of the Callander & Oban. Temporary termini were established at Tyndrum and Dalmally

before the route was totally complete. That it was ever finished at all owes much to the railway's energetic manager, John Anderson, who at one point had to tour the area like a door to door salesman in order to raise enough funds to keep the project moving forward. Appointed secretary of the company in 1865, he didn't retire until 1907. Perhaps he would have been proud to see his railway fully integrated with the West Highland and surviving into the 21st century; perhaps he would have regretted the sacrifice of its original approach from Stirling and Callander.

2001 is the Mallaig Extension's centenary. It's been lucky to survive Beeching and Serpell into an era where railways are recognised as being both environmentally and socially desirable means of transport. Heaven help the politician or accountant who dared suggest abandoning the West Highland Lines today; though that's not to say that 'market forces' couldn't bring about the downfall of such a railway in the sort of extreme circumstances witnessed after the Hatfield incident of late 2000. Hitherto, freight has kept the lines intact. It should continue to do so, though it is not without its own uncertainties: the right wagons, the right locomotives, the right traffic flows; the ability to match price with performance against the insidious advance of the juggernaut. Good news comes from Grangemouth, where improved rail connections should result in oil traffic returning to West Highland rail-linked depots at Connel Ferry and Fort William.

AND are the West Highland Lines recognisably the railways that they were built to be? In broad transport terms they are; though it's amusing to consider that no amount of new technology has ever brought about a significant reduction in schedules. Railway enthusiasts will tell you that things aren't what they used to be. They mourn the more obvious trappings of a thoroughgoing railway: staffed stations, goods yards, semaphore signals, locomotive-hauled trains as opposed to Sprinter units, restaurant cars, and those glorious manifestations of the post-war West Highland heyday, the observation car.

GENERATIONS of classic West Highland motive power have left an indelible mark in the memories of those who love the line. A time traveller would be hard put to chose a 'desert island' selection of favourite classes: Reid's elegant Glen 4-4-0s; Gresley's lovely, Scottish-named, Doncaster and Darlington made Moguls of classes K2 and K4; and the ubiquitous Stanier Black 5s, indigenous to the Oban line as well. Even diesel designs have their followers: the unreliable but characterful Glasgow-built North British Bo-Bos, and their more successful Smethwick-built BRCW counterparts; and the rugged-looking, bonnet-nosed English Electric Class 37s which had almost a monopoly on West Highland passenger and freight services throughout the Eighties, and of which one or two remain, essential for requirements into the foreseeable future.

Crianlarich on a winter's evening.

AND a wish list for the future? Something more substantial for the summer season than the sometimes overburdened Sprinters; something with a bit of swagger about it. A Scottish Parliament sponsored train perhaps, a tub-thumping exponent of Caledonian pride, with real rolling stock - a restaurant car serving the best of Scots cuisine, an observation carriage with an accordionist, and a guards van with room not only for the carriage of bicycles but their hiring-out as well. A couple of Class 27s purring away up front in tartan livery. The West Highland Lines are up there with the world's most beautiful railways and deserve a bit more than a bus on wheels to do their rugged landscapes justice.

TO make the most of the line's potential for tourism, the North British Railway commissioned a guide book from the London publishing firm of Joseph Causton & Sons. Publication of the richly illustrated hardback, which ran to 178 pages and which was typically effusive of text for its time, coincided with the opening of the line to Fort William in 1894. A pre-publication copy was forwarded to Queen Victoria in the hope that she would consent to open the line. It would have been a coup for the railway company to secure the Queen's patronage, especially as they were still trying to obtain an Act of Parliament for the line's Extension beyond Fort William and the Lochaber district to the West Coast. In the event the railway travelling monarch was not sufficiently amused by the prospect to grace the opening ceremony with her presence, but the guide book, resonantly titled Mountain Moor & Loch went on to sell fourteen thousand copies in its first year and ten thousand the next.

I would be thrilled (and so would my wife, my bank manager, and those nice people in Cumbernauld who are always dropping me a line) if this guide book could emulate those sales figures. Like Mountain Moor & Loch all those years ago, it is designed to whet your appetite to travel over the West Highland Lines; to act as a mildly informative, entertaining and not too overpowering companion on your journey; and to be a valued souvenir of what hopefully will have been a memorable and enjoyable experience. Have fun, I wish I was coming with you!

Michael Pearson

ACKNOWLEDGEMENTS

Fundamentals first! This guide would not have taken shape in any form whatsoever without the indefatigable stewardship of Mr John Yellowlees, External Relations Manager of ScotRail. For it was he who, single-handedly, snatched opportunity from the dripping fangs of defeat, when our original concept for a coffee-table book devoted to the whole of Scotland's scenic railways derailed in the rusty sidings of a petrified forest of denuded budgets - the like of which, many believe, lies at the end of the line of privatisation in its present form. Mr Yellowlees' enthusiasm galvanised moral and fiscal support from many angles, alphabetically acknowledged as follows: John Allison (Highland Council); John Barnes (Friends of the West Highland Lines & Glenfinnan Station Museum); Alison Brawn (Freightliner); Evelyn Brown (Railtrack); Beverley Cole (National Railway Museum); Sue Evans (EWS); Geoffrey Evison (Friends of Riccarton Junction); Dr. Bob Gardner (Friends of the West Highland Lines); Paul Henning (Alcan); Chris Hogg (National Railway Museum); John Hynds (ScotRail); Andy Lickfold (EWS); John Lone (ScotRail); Dr. John McGregor; Arnold Macbeth (ScotRail); Duncan MacLean (ScotRail); Ian McCulloch (Alcan); Marie MacKay (Alcan); Graham Meiklejohn (EWS); Lynn Patrick (National Railway Museum); Roy Pedersen and Ken Porter (Highlands & Islands Enterprise); Malcolm C. Reed (Strathclyde Passenger Transport); Frank Roach (Highland Rail Partnership); Carrie Robb (ScotRail); James Shuttleworth (West Coast Railway Co.); Eddie Toal (ScotRail); Iain Tod (EWS); Andy Thomas (ScotRail); Ken Vickers (Cordee); Steve Webb (Nexus). Special thanks must go to: Karen Tanguy of Wayzgoose for her unstinting help in the production of this guide; and to the author's family for putting up with all his absences and his comings and goings in the 'wee sma 'oors' on his way to and from Crewe station.

PHOTOGRAPHS

Grateful thanks to all the photographers who helped fill the gaps the author was unable, for one reason or another - mostly the unforgiving minutes and the unforgiving elements - to attend to: Phil Connell of Bishopbriggs; Dennis & Tony Hardley of Benderloch; Chris Hogg & Lynn Patrick of the National Railway Museum; Peter J. Robinson of Tynemouth; James Shuttleworth of Hathersage; Allan Wright of Castle Douglas. The uncaptioned cover and title page photographs are as follows: *Front cover:* Dennis Hardley's spectacular wide angle view of the Horseshoe Viaduct at Auch; *rear cover:* James Shuttleworth's atmospherically snowbound Beinn Dorain; *title page:* Dennis Hardley's quintessential Rathad Iarainn Nan Eilean view of the track of the Mallaig Extension at Glenfinnan.

Rannoch station footbridge.

LOCH LOMOND **LMS**
LNER
SCOTLAND FOR HOLIDAYS

GLASGOW &
FORT WILLIAM

Achallader

Loch Lomond

Peter J. Robinson

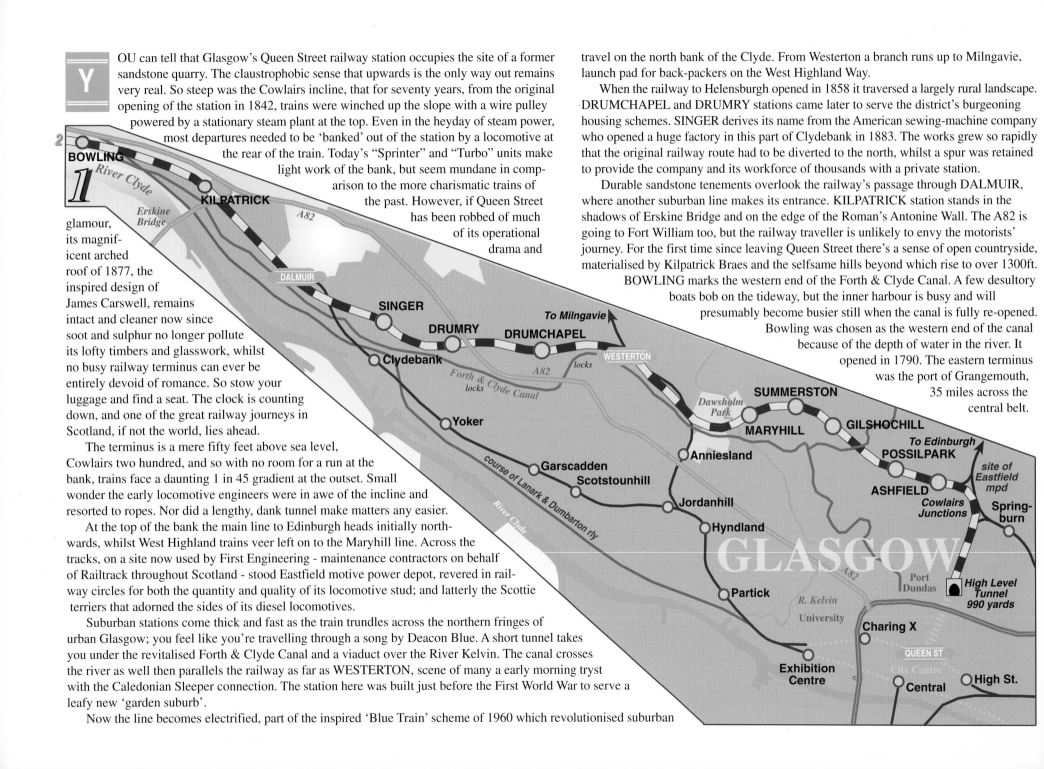

YOU can tell that Glasgow's Queen Street railway station occupies the site of a former sandstone quarry. The claustrophobic sense that upwards is the only way out remains very real. So steep was the Cowlairs incline, that for seventy years, from the original opening of the station in 1842, trains were winched up the slope with a wire pulley powered by a stationary steam plant at the top. Even in the heyday of steam power, most departures needed to be 'banked' out of the station by a locomotive at the rear of the train. Today's "Sprinter" and "Turbo" units make light work of the bank, but seem mundane in comparison to the more charismatic trains of the past. However, if Queen Street has been robbed of much of its operational drama and glamour, its magnificent arched roof of 1877, the inspired design of James Carswell, remains intact and cleaner now since soot and sulphur no longer pollute its lofty timbers and glasswork, whilst no busy railway terminus can ever be entirely devoid of romance. So stow your luggage and find a seat. The clock is counting down, and one of the great railway journeys in Scotland, if not the world, lies ahead.

The terminus is a mere fifty feet above sea level, Cowlairs two hundred, and so with no room for a run at the bank, trains face a daunting 1 in 45 gradient at the outset. Small wonder the early locomotive engineers were in awe of the incline and resorted to ropes. Nor did a lengthy, dank tunnel make matters any easier.

At the top of the bank the main line to Edinburgh heads initially northwards, whilst West Highland trains veer left on to the Maryhill line. Across the tracks, on a site now used by First Engineering - maintenance contractors on behalf of Railtrack throughout Scotland - stood Eastfield motive power depot, revered in railway circles for both the quantity and quality of its locomotive stud; and latterly the Scottie terriers that adorned the sides of its diesel locomotives.

Suburban stations come thick and fast as the train trundles across the northern fringes of urban Glasgow; you feel like you're travelling through a song by Deacon Blue. A short tunnel takes you under the revitalised Forth & Clyde Canal and a viaduct over the River Kelvin. The canal crosses the river as well then parallels the railway as far as WESTERTON, scene of many a early morning tryst with the Caledonian Sleeper connection. The station here was built just before the First World War to serve a leafy new 'garden suburb'.

Now the line becomes electrified, part of the inspired 'Blue Train' scheme of 1960 which revolutionised suburban

travel on the north bank of the Clyde. From Westerton a branch runs up to Milngavie, launch pad for back-packers on the West Highland Way.

When the railway to Helensburgh opened in 1858 it traversed a largely rural landscape. DRUMCHAPEL and DRUMRY stations came later to serve the district's burgeoning housing schemes. SINGER derives its name from the American sewing-machine company who opened a huge factory in this part of Clydebank in 1883. The works grew so rapidly that the original railway route had to be diverted to the north, whilst a spur was retained to provide the company and its workforce of thousands with a private station.

Durable sandstone tenements overlook the railway's passage through DALMUIR, where another suburban line makes its entrance. KILPATRICK station stands in the shadows of Erskine Bridge and on the edge of the Roman's Antonine Wall. The A82 is going to Fort William too, but the railway traveller is unlikely to envy the motorists' journey. For the first time since leaving Queen Street there's a sense of open countryside, materialised by Kilpatrick Braes and the selfsame hills beyond which rise to over 1300ft. BOWLING marks the western end of the Forth & Clyde Canal. A few desultory boats bob on the tideway, but the inner harbour is busy and will presumably become busier still when the canal is fully re-opened. Bowling was chosen as the western end of the canal because of the depth of water in the river. It opened in 1790. The eastern terminus was the port of Grangemouth, 35 miles across the central belt.

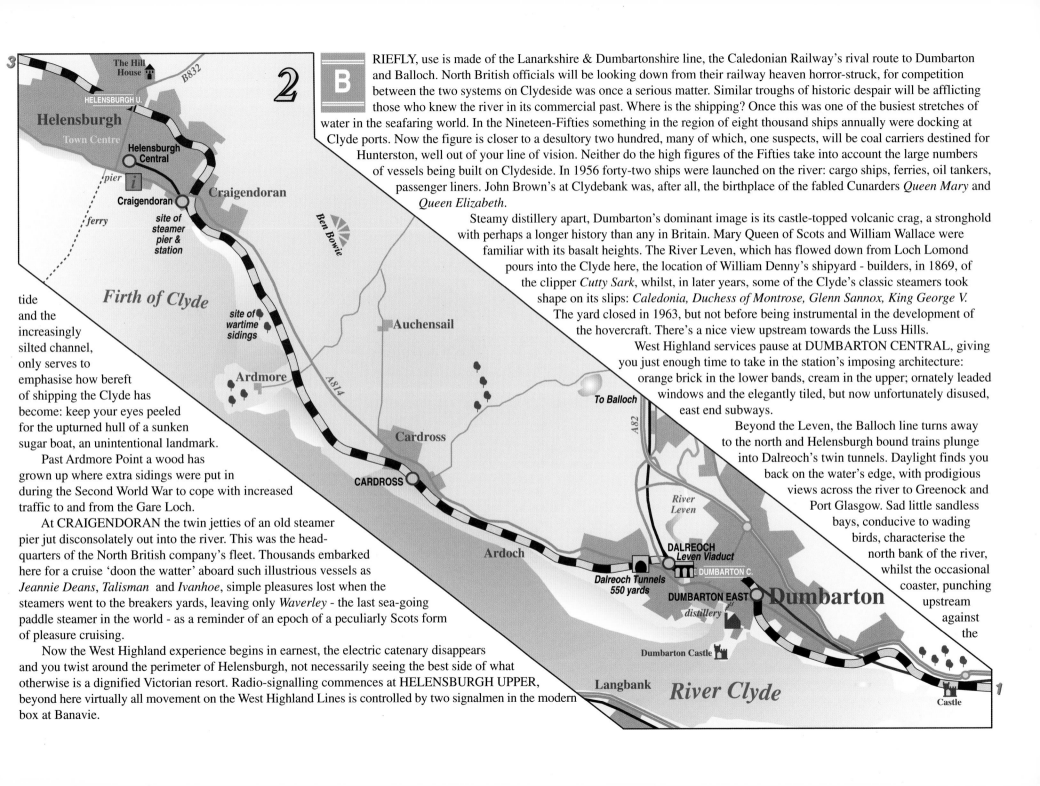

3

2

The Hill House

B832

HELENSBURGH U.

Helensburgh

Town Centre

Helensburgh Central

pier

i

Craigendoran

Craigendoran

ferry

site of steamer pier & station

Ben Bowie

Firth of Clyde

site of wartime sidings

Auchensail

Ardmore

A814

tide
and the
increasingly
silted channel,
only serves to
emphasise how bereft
of shipping the Clyde has
become: keep your eyes peeled
for the upturned hull of a sunken
sugar boat, an unintentional landmark.

Past Ardmore Point a wood has
grown up where extra sidings were put in
during the Second World War to cope with increased
traffic to and from the Gare Loch.

At CRAIGENDORAN the twin jetties of an old steamer
pier jut disconsolately out into the river. This was the head-
quarters of the North British company's fleet. Thousands embarked
here for a cruise 'doon the watter' aboard such illustrious vessels as
Jeannie Deans, *Talisman* and *Ivanhoe*, simple pleasures lost when the
steamers went to the breakers yards, leaving only *Waverley* - the last sea-going
paddle steamer in the world - as a reminder of an epoch of a peculiarly Scots form
of pleasure cruising.

Now the West Highland experience begins in earnest, the electric catenary disappears
and you twist around the perimeter of Helensburgh, not necessarily seeing the best side of what
otherwise is a dignified Victorian resort. Radio-signalling commences at HELENSBURGH UPPER,
beyond here virtually all movement on the West Highland Lines is controlled by two signalmen in the modern
box at Banavie.

Cardross

CARDROSS

Ardoch

B

RIEFLY, use is made of the Lanarkshire & Dumbartonshire line, the Caledonian Railway's rival route to Dumbarton
and Balloch. North British officials will be looking down from their railway heaven horror-struck, for competition
between the two systems on Clydeside was once a serious matter. Similar troughs of historic despair will be afflicting
those who knew the river in its commercial past. Where is the shipping? Once this was one of the busiest stretches of
water in the seafaring world. In the Nineteen-Fifties something in the region of eight thousand ships annually were docking at
Clyde ports. Now the figure is closer to a desultory two hundred, many of which, one suspects, will be coal carriers destined for
Hunterston, well out of your line of vision. Neither do the high figures of the Fifties take into account the large numbers
of vessels being built on Clydeside. In 1956 forty-two ships were launched on the river: cargo ships, ferries, oil tankers,
passenger liners. John Brown's at Clydebank was, after all, the birthplace of the fabled Cunarders *Queen Mary* and
Queen Elizabeth.

Steamy distillery apart, Dumbarton's dominant image is its castle-topped volcanic crag, a stronghold
with perhaps a longer history than any in Britain. Mary Queen of Scots and William Wallace were
familiar with its basalt heights. The River Leven, which has flowed down from Loch Lomond
pours into the Clyde here, the location of William Denny's shipyard - builders, in 1869, of
the clipper *Cutty Sark*, whilst, in later years, some of the Clyde's classic steamers took
shape on its slips: *Caledonia, Duchess of Montrose, Glenn Sannox, King George V.*
The yard closed in 1963, but not before being instrumental in the development of
the hovercraft. There's a nice view upstream towards the Luss Hills.

West Highland services pause at DUMBARTON CENTRAL, giving
you just enough time to take in the station's imposing architecture:
orange brick in the lower bands, cream in the upper; ornately leaded
windows and the elegantly tiled, but now unfortunately disused,
east end subways.

Beyond the Leven, the Balloch line turns away
to the north and Helensburgh bound trains plunge
into Dalreoch's twin tunnels. Daylight finds you
back on the water's edge, with prodigious
views across the river to Greenock and
Port Glasgow. Sad little sandless
bays, conducive to wading
birds, characterise the
north bank of the river,
whilst the occasional
coaster, punching
upstream
against
the

To Balloch

A82

River Leven

DALREOCH
Leven Viaduct

DUMBARTON C.

Dalreoch Tunnels
550 yards

DUMBARTON EAST

Dumbarton

distillery

Dumbarton Castle

Langbank

River Clyde

1

Castle

THREE-QUARTERS of an hour after leaving Glasgow the show is about to begin. You feel as though you've been warmed up by an enjoyable support act but now you can hardly contain your excitement as the line runs on a ledge along the hillside overlooking Gare Loch and the spectacular scenery of the highlands begins to manifest itself. The Highland Boundary Fault, the result of a bit of an altercation between two rock masses four hundred million years ago, brings about this sudden scene change: the malleable red sandstone from which all those Clydeside towns built their tenements gives way to the more recalcitrant and brittle rocks of the north-west.

In the mid 19th century Glasgow's more prosperous gentry were erecting sizeable mansions along the bonny banks of the Gare Loch. Robert Napier, the shipbuilder and close friend of David Livingstone the explorer, built a sizeable house here in 1846 which, after his death, became a Hydro. The North British Railway Company had high hopes of developing this trade, bringing the area within the expanding pockets of the burgeoning middle classes. Suburban stations were erected at Rhu (formerly known as Row), Shandon, Garelochhead and Whistlefield for what became referred to as the 'villa' traffic. Unfortunately, they were mostly an ill-sited, steep walk from the lochside areas of housing, and never really took off. So of these optimistic halts, only GARE-LOCHHEAD remains open; saved, no doubt, by the trade in matelots and submariners. A service of stopping trains operated between Craigendoran and Arrochar & Tarbet until as surprisingly late as 1964. Towards the end a four-wheel Wickham railbus sufficed for the dwindling clientele, prior to that the timetable had been elegantly operated by Willy Reid's elegant 4-4-2 tank locomotives with a couple of wooden-bodied carriages in push & pull mode.

Up until the 19th century Gare Loch was a quiet backwater not unknown in whisky smuggling circles. As vessels grew in size the loch became recognised as a prime anchorage, coming into its own in wartime. A double track branch was laid down to the Admiralty port of Faslane (aka Military Port No.1) opening under a cloak of secrecy in 1943. The line was worked by War Department staff on European principals, the idea being that it would provide good training for personnel as D-Day approached. A platform was provided dockside for troop movements. One of the first people to use it was Winston Churchill on his way across the Atlantic for a tete-a-tete with Teddy Roosevelt.

After the war Gare Loch became better known as a centre for ship-breaking, the branch line was demilitarised and busied itself with scrap. Then, more sinisterly in some eyes, the name Faslane grew to

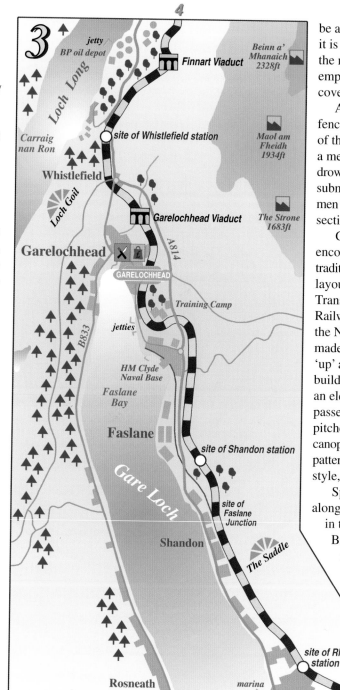

be associated with Britain's nuclear deterrent. Nowadays it is known as the HM Naval Base Clyde and, whatever the moral rights or wrongs of its function, it is a huge employer on a site dominated by the massive bulk of a covered shiplift.

A sharp S-bend carries the railway past the high security fences of a Ministry of Defence training camp. At the foot of the embankment lies Faslane Cemetery which contains a memorial to eighty-three submariners and civilians drowned in an acceptance trial for the steam turbine powered submarine *K13* on 29th January 1917. Happily, forty-eight men trapped for nearly three days in the submarine's forward section were subsequently saved.

GARELOCHHEAD is the northbound traveller's first encounter with one of the West Highland Railway's traditional 'Swiss-style' station buildings and island platform layout. It also marks the end of Strathclyde Passenger Transport territory. In common with the Great Central Railway's London Extension at the end of the 19th century, the North British company recognised the savings to be made in eschewing the traditional provision of separate 'up' and 'down' platforms and the inherent duplication of buildings. Approached via a subway, which slopes up to an elegant pair of wrought iron gates, the prospective passenger encounters a single storey building: a split-pitched overhanging roof avoids the need for separate canopies; a brick base contrasts with upper panels of shingle-patterned timber. This is the West Highland's 'Swiss chalet' style, a leitmotif for much of your journey.

Sprung points - as you will see on several occasions along the line - have the peculiar effect of routing trains in the opposite direction to that usually encountered on Britain's railways where, in common with our roads, it is the practice to travel on the left: ease of access to the sidings brought about this anomaly. From Garelochhead viaduct there's a tantalising view westwards up Loch Goil. Down through the trees lies Loch Long and BP's Finnart Ocean Terminal, linked by pipeline to the famous refinery at Grangemouth. Crude oil is imported by tanker ship and finished products exported.

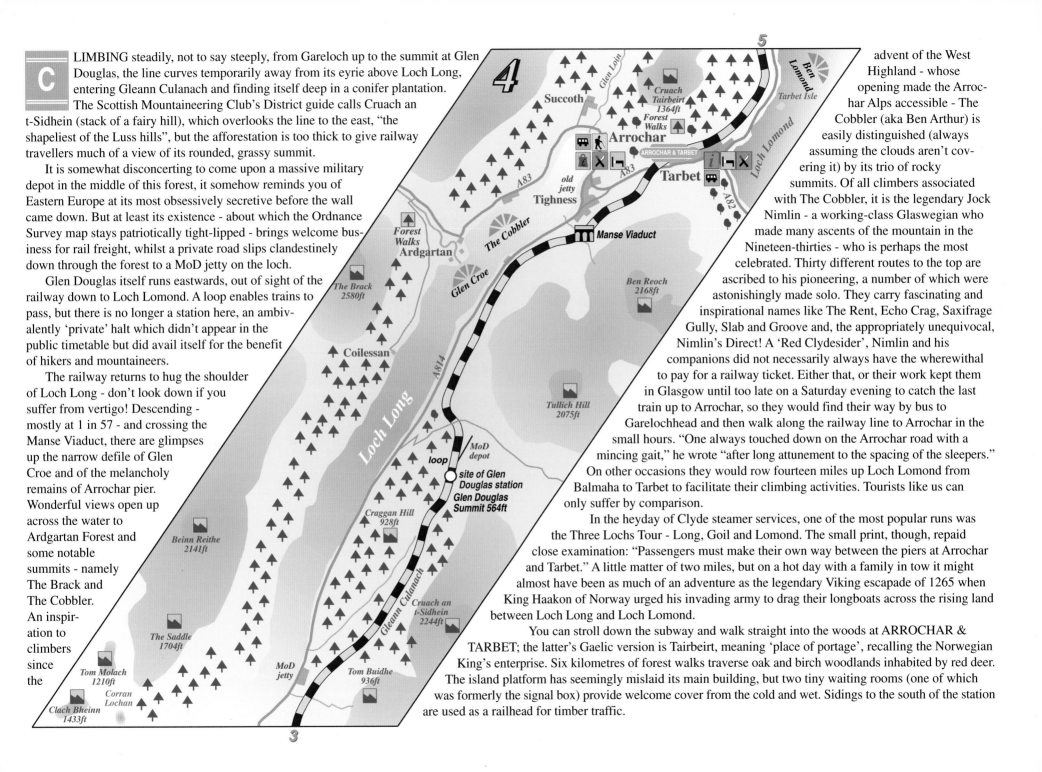

LIMBING steadily, not to say steeply, from Gareloch up to the summit at Glen Douglas, the line curves temporarily away from its eyrie above Loch Long, entering Gleann Culanach and finding itself deep in a conifer plantation. The Scottish Mountaineering Club's District guide calls Cruach an t-Sidhein (stack of a fairy hill), which overlooks the line to the east, "the shapeliest of the Luss hills", but the afforestation is too thick to give railway travellers much of a view of its rounded, grassy summit.

It is somewhat disconcerting to come upon a massive military depot in the middle of this forest, it somehow reminds you of Eastern Europe at its most obsessively secretive before the wall came down. But at least its existence - about which the Ordnance Survey map stays patriotically tight-lipped - brings welcome business for rail freight, whilst a private road slips clandestinely down through the forest to a MoD jetty on the loch.

Glen Douglas itself runs eastwards, out of sight of the railway down to Loch Lomond. A loop enables trains to pass, but there is no longer a station here, an ambivalently 'private' halt which didn't appear in the public timetable but did avail itself for the benefit of hikers and mountaineers.

The railway returns to hug the shoulder of Loch Long - don't look down if you suffer from vertigo! Descending - mostly at 1 in 57 - and crossing the Manse Viaduct, there are glimpses up the narrow defile of Glen Croe and of the melancholy remains of Arrochar pier. Wonderful views open up across the water to Ardgartan Forest and some notable summits - namely The Brack and The Cobbler. An inspiration to climbers since the

advent of the West Highland - whose opening made the Arrochar Alps accessible - The Cobbler (aka Ben Arthur) is easily distinguished (always assuming the clouds aren't covering it) by its trio of rocky summits. Of all climbers associated with The Cobbler, it is the legendary Jock Nimlin - a working-class Glaswegian who made many ascents of the mountain in the Nineteen-thirties - who is perhaps the most celebrated. Thirty different routes to the top are ascribed to his pioneering, a number of which were astonishingly made solo. They carry fascinating and inspirational names like The Rent, Echo Crag, Saxifrage Gully, Slab and Groove and, the appropriately unequivocal, Nimlin's Direct! A 'Red Clydesider', Nimlin and his companions did not necessarily always have the wherewithal to pay for a railway ticket. Either that, or their work kept them in Glasgow until too late on a Saturday evening to catch the last train up to Arrochar, so they would find their way by bus to Garelochhead and then walk along the railway line to Arrochar in the small hours. "One always touched down on the Arrochar road with a mincing gait," he wrote "after long attunement to the spacing of the sleepers." On other occasions they would row fourteen miles up Loch Lomond from Balmaha to Tarbet to facilitate their climbing activities. Tourists like us can only suffer by comparison.

In the heyday of Clyde steamer services, one of the most popular runs was the Three Lochs Tour - Long, Goil and Lomond. The small print, though, repaid close examination: "Passengers must make their own way between the piers at Arrochar and Tarbet." A little matter of two miles, but on a hot day with a family in tow it might almost have been as much of an adventure as the legendary Viking escapade of 1265 when King Haakon of Norway urged his invading army to drag their longboats across the rising land between Loch Long and Loch Lomond.

You can stroll down the subway and walk straight into the woods at ARROCHAR & TARBET; the latter's Gaelic version is Tairbeirt, meaning 'place of portage', recalling the Norwegian King's enterprise. Six kilometres of forest walks traverse oak and birch woodlands inhabited by red deer. The island platform has seemingly mislaid its main building, but two tiny waiting rooms (one of which was formerly the signal box) provide welcome cover from the cold and wet. Sidings to the south of the station are used as a railhead for timber traffic.

Map labels:

4

5

Glen Loin

Ben Lomond

Tarbet Isle

Succoth

Cruach Tairbeirt 1364ft

Forest Walks

Arrochar

ARROCHAR & TARBET

Loch Lomond

Tarbet

old jetty

Tighness

A83

A83

A82

Forest Walks

Ardgartan

The Cobbler

Manse Viaduct

Glen Croe

The Brack 2580ft

Ben Reoch 2168ft

Coilessan

A814

Loch Long

Tullich Hill 2075ft

loop

MoD depot

site of Glen Douglas station

Glen Douglas Summit 564ft

Craggan Hill 928ft

Beinn Reithe 2141ft

Gleann Culanach

Cruach an t-Sidhein 2244ft

The Saddle 1704ft

MoD jetty

Tom Buidhe 936ft

Tom Molach 1210ft

Corran Lochan

Clach Bheinn 1433ft

3

LOCH LOMOND, Britain's biggest body of inland water, provides rail travellers with a fresh focus of interest as the West Highland hugs its western banks for almost ten extravagantly scenic miles. 2001 marks the recognition of Loch Lomond and The Trossachs as Scotland's first National Park. The North British and London & North Eastern railway companies, together with British Railways in the Nineteen-fifties, celebrated Loch Lomond, and the neighbouring Trossachs, in a series of remarkable posters featuring the work of well established artists such as Tom Purvis, Keith Henderson and J. Macintosh Patrick. In hindsight their work wears its heart on its sleeve, presenting a romantic, stylised interpretation of this landscape which modern, photograph-based tourist images cannot equal. Enjoying them now, you yearn for an era of such innocence, whether it ever existed or not. Loch Lomond's most famous song lyric is apt to have the same effect on you. "Oh ye'll tak' the high road and I'll tak' the low road" is said to reflect the fate of two of Bonnie Prince Charlie's men captured in Carlisle after the failure of the '45 rebellion. One was to be executed, the other released. The spirit of the dead soldier, travelling by the 'low road', would reach Scotland before his comrade who faced a long walk home.

After Ben Nevis, Ben Lomond is probably the best known mountain in Scotland, certainly as far as the man in the street is concerned; the climbing fraternity own to many other esoteric favourites. At 3192ft above sea level it is the most southerly of the Munros. The name derives from an old term for beacon, a description it fulfils more than adequately as its summit towers almost conically above the eastern side of the loch. The most popular route for an ascent of Ben Lomond is from Rowardennan on the east bank of Loch Lomond.

Loch Lomondside is well known as Rob Roy country. The red-headed MacGregor bandit was a sort of Scottish Robin Hood, whose otherwise nefarious activities were much romanticised by Sir Walter Scott. Born in 1670, Rob Roy was an educated man as well as a warrior. He set much store by the Highland way of life and tradition and in many respects it ran contrary to his character to be a cattle rustler and bandit, for amongst his peers he was regarded as a fair and honest businessman. With his red hair and fair complexion he became a figurehead intent on maintaining the clan system. In 1715 he allied his clan to the Jacobite cause and was charged with treason.

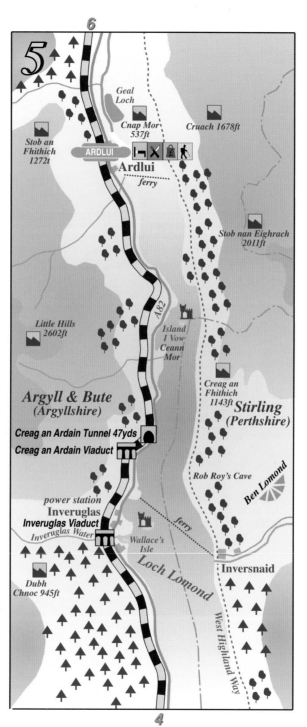

For the next twenty years he lived the life of an outlaw, narrowly escaping capture on many occasions. He died at the age of 63 and is buried in Balquhidder churchyard.

The railway switchbacks along the bank of the loch, woodland for much of the time, masking the best views. A useful halt was opened in the vicinity of Inveruglas in 1945, mainly for the use of workmen (many of whom were prisoners of war) involved in the nearby Loch Sloy hydro-electric power scheme. Four massive pipes make a spectacular descent of the hillside to reach the power station, a not unhandsome building containing turbines by the lochside.

Built in 1894 and listed Grade B, Creag an Ardain Viaduct is the only conventionally built masonry viaduct on the West Highland Railway, the line's engineers preferring to use prefabricated metal structures in most locations, but upping the aesthetic ante here in response to the proximity of the peerless loch. Frustratingly, an overabundance of vegetation diminishes its standing in the landscape, a shame this, because the designers went to town with battlemented parapets and craggy spandrels to its nine arches. Inveruglas was one of five locations where the line's builders established camps. Materials were delivered by barge to a specially built pier on the lochside - before completion of the railway there would have been no other effective means of transport to so remote a tract of country.

So Loch Lomond played its part in the railway's existence both prior and subsequent to its opening. Travel blossomed and steamer services on the loch interconnected with trains for what, in retrospect, became a golden era of tourism which flourished, like many aspects of British holidaymaking, until mass motoring in the Nineteen Sixties brought it to an abrupt end. The steamer pier at Ardlui was closed in 1964. Duncan Graham describes it evocatively in *Sunset on the Clyde* his entertaining memories of life as a student purser on Loch Lomond and the Clyde in the Nineteen-fifties and sixties. He spent his time on Loch Lomond on the paddle steamer *Maid of the Loch*, the largest ever inland cruising vessel built in Britain. Launched in 1953, she belonged to a better age, and became, as Graham so eloquently puts it "a victim of accountancy". Out of use since 1981, several abortive attempts have been made to restore her and one can only hope the latest initiative proves successful.

The traditional, but subsidence-ridden, West Highland station buildings at ARDLUI have been demolished.

T HE lochs are left behind as the railway begins to climb into a wilder, mountainous region. The inn at Inverarnan played host to the project's engineers when the line was being constructed. Later the River Falloch was dredged, a basin dug and a short canal constructed so that steamers could reach beyond the head of Loch Lomond. Prior to the coming of the railway, horse-drawn coaches would carry travellers up over the mountains on the old military road to the north. The inn's pedigree is a long one, going back to cattle droving days. Later it became a favoured centre of accommodation for climbers.

You are entering waterfall country where, especially after periods of heavy rainfall, a sequence of torrents hurl themselves like demented abseilers off the hillsides down into the glen. Largest of the Falloch's tributaries, the Dubh Eas (or Black Water) cascades down beneath the lofty, 143ft high, Glen Falloch Viaduct, a typical West Highland structure of concrete piers and steel trusses. As the railway climbs, so the forestry thins. Here and there, though, on the increasingly bare moorland are isolated pines, remnants of a huge forest which long ago covered this wilderness. Laterally, they remind you of the shipyard cranes back at Clydebank, similarly denuded by the passage of time.

Some serious climbing ensues, the train being faced with an ascent of over five hundred feet in five miles to reach Crianlarich. At times the gradient is as steep as 1 in 60: in other words, if you're locomotive-hauled and the windows are down, the sounds of some serious 'thrash' being given to the traction will be wafting through Glen Falloch. Aboard one of the ubiquitous Sprinters which make up most of the services on the line the effect is not quite so pyrotechnic, but you will still hear the underfloor engines straining against the grade in the northbound direction. It must have been marvellous in steam days with, say, a pair of 'Glens' at the head of your train, barking their way vociferously onwards and upwards as the line twisted and turned with the craggy contours of the narrowing glen.

The top of the glen marks the watershed between eastern and western Scotland. Water in the Falloch finds it way to the Clyde; the River Fillan which flows through Crianlarich is a once-removed tributary of the Tay. Trundling down into Crianlarich, there's a real sense that a new chapter in the journey is about to begin. Queen Street is sixty miles behind you in railway terms, but a world away in atmosphere.

CRIANLARICH reminds you of one of those classic country junctions created, not so much with custom in mind, but out of railway operating expedience: another Melton Constable, another Halwill, another (should you insist on a Scots analogy) Cairnie Junction. It is a welcome survival, there are not many places left in Britain - though examples still thrive abroad - where portions of trains are split or joined and a goods yard still shunted for profit - timber again. Furthermore, First Engineering use the former engine shed ("lovely" and "chapel-like" according to Alexander Frater's enjoyable collection of railway journeys *Stopping Train Britain*) as accommodation for sundry maintenance vehicles, which adds to the sense of activity in the exquisite wood-smoke-scented silence between trains.

Breakfast and luncheon baskets traditionally greeted famished passengers at Crianlarich. One drools at the thought of wicker hampers filled with glazed delights awaiting intrepid Edwardian travellers; and while passengers gobbled down their picnics, the engines took on water. The present-day proprietors of the station tearoom, Mr and Mrs Cull, do their best to uphold the service in these less extravagant times.

Delving deeply into the railway history of this part of the world, you discover that Crianlarich only really acquired junction status in 1965. Prior to that it was the point at which the West Highland Railway of 1894 crossed over the Callander & Oban Railway which had brought the sounds and smells of a working railway to Strath Fillan twenty years earlier. For eighty-five years the two lines were effectively worked as separate entities, notwithstanding the existence of a linking chord put in place to facilitate the exchange of goods traffic. This spur finally came into its own when the C&O was blocked east of Crianlarich by a rockfall, though nature was only accelerating what Beeching had already planned. In the road traffic orientated second half of the twentieth century it made irrefutable economic sense to concentrate services between Glasgow and Oban on the seventeen miles shorter West Highland route, even if a beautiful length of railway was lost in the process. You only have to drive along the A85, through the rocky defile of Glen Ogle, catching tantalising glimpses of the abandoned trackbed and its bridges and viaducts to appreciate what a lovely line it must have been. But then lost lines, by definition, are invariably the ones that tug most achingly at your heartstrings.

Map labels

6

A82

River Fillan

Inverhaggernie Viaduct

Crianlarich & Fillan Viaducts

Ben More

CRIANLARICH

Crianlarich

Craw Knowe 1523ft

Old Military Road

Ben Challum

A82

River Falloch

Glen Falloch

West Highland Way

Ben Chabhair

Glen Falloch Viaduct

Falls of Falloch

Dubh Eas

Ben Glas

Inverarnan

Stirling (Perthshire)

Argyll & Bute (Argyllshire)

RUNNING independently through Strath Fillan as far as Tyndrum, the Fort William and Oban lines begin to climb to their respective summits, more dramatically in the former case to reach over a thousand feet at County March. Often you will see the other portion of your train threading its parallel course through the valley. It's an enjoyable and intriguing sight even in the age of the Sprinter, for in ScotRail's purple, green and orange colour scheme the units can look very attractive across the silvery waters of the River Fillan. That's not to say, though, that part of you doesn't wish away the years to a previous era of privatised railways. Diligent reference to a 1922 Bradshaw, for example, will reveal that, between 1.45 and 2pm, if running to schedule, the 11.35am from Queen Street to Mallaig would be traversing the North British line at the same time as the 12.10pm from Oban was making its way to Glasgow Buchanan Street by way of Callander and Stirling. What an encounter that would have been, the North British Railway's West Highland train in what railway writer Hamilton Ellis referred to as "a rather flat purplish red" with a brown locomotive at its head; the Caledonian Railway's Callander & Oban train in brown and white, its engine Prussian blue.

Strath Fillan's use as a thoroughfare goes back a long way. In the eighteenth century General Caulfield took advantage of its easy going acres to extend the military road system from Stirling to Fort William, whilst prior to that Tyndrum was at the meeting place of drove roads from the west and north. The Scots engineer Thomas Telford was commissioned to improve the road system of the Highlands at the beginning of the 19th century. A busy man - he was also building the Ellesmere Canal in Shropshire - he drove himself hard to complete his initial reconnaissance: "I have carried regular surveys along the rainy west through the middle of the tempestuous wilds of Lochaber. The apprehension of the weather changing for the worse has prompted me to incessant hard labour so that I am almost lame and blind." Telford was also charged with finding out reasons for a great exodus taking place in the Highlands at the time. He didn't need to look far. The landowners of the region found the rearing of sheep more profitable than crofting. Like the Romans before him, Telford argued that improved communications could only have a beneficial effect on the economy.

Of course the valley's history goes back much further than the provision of recognisable roads. St Fillan is said to have journeyed down the glen from Iona and established a chapel here in the 8th century. The site gained priory status in the 14th century,

though little now remains other than an interpretive board on the West Highland Way. From the passing train it is Kirkton Farm and its outbuildings which catches the eye, look out for the small hillside cemetery with its two yew trees, resting place of generations of local farmers. Not only is the luxuriant valley of the River Fillan associated with agriculture. In the 15th century Tyndrum boasted a silver mine. More recently the flanks of Meall Odhar were worked for lead, the scars of this activity have never fully healed.

UPPER TYNDRUM is aptly named, for the West Highland station stands a steep, hairpin, helter-skelter track above the community it serves. Originally this perfectly preserved (though sadly empty) station was known as Tyndrum Upper, but when the two lines were radio-signalled in 1988 the name was reversed to avoid confusion. In contrast, TYNDRUM LOWER has lost all its former buildings and stands with bus-sheltered simplicity at the other end of the village.

Climbing at 1 in 60 out of Tyndrum, the West Highland Railway reaches County March Summit, entering a landscape with an increased sense of wildness about it, as emphasised by the snow posts on the adjoining A82.

In steam days the fireman might have been tempted to rest on his laurels as the train dropped down the succeeding 1 in 55 and gingerly found its way around the celebrated Horseshoe Curve under the twin peaks of Odhar and Dorain. Had the budget not been so tight, the railway might have taken a more direct course, crossing the meeting of the glens on a lengthy viaduct, but had it done so, us tourists would have lost one of the line's most endearing features. Look out for the surfaceman's house to the north of the line by Gleann Viaduct and imagine how austere life must have been for the railwayman and his family.

Map labels

West Highland Way
B8074
Glen Orchy
A82
Old Military Road
Beinn Dorain 3524ft
Auch Gleann
Auch
Horseshoe Viaduct
Beinn a' Chaisteil 2897ft
Gleann Viaduct
Glen Coralan
Beinn Odhar 2948ft
Argyll & Bute (Argyllshire)
County March Summit 1024ft
Stirling (Perthshire)
Beinn Chaorach 2655ft
Beinn Bheag 2149ft
Tyndrum Summit 840ft
Meall Buidhe 2136ft
Lochan na Bi
A85
UPPER TYNDRUM
TYNDRUM LOWER
An Caisteal
Meall Odhar 2150ft
Tyndrum
Auchtertyre Viaduct
wigwams
Cononish Viaduct
St Fillan's

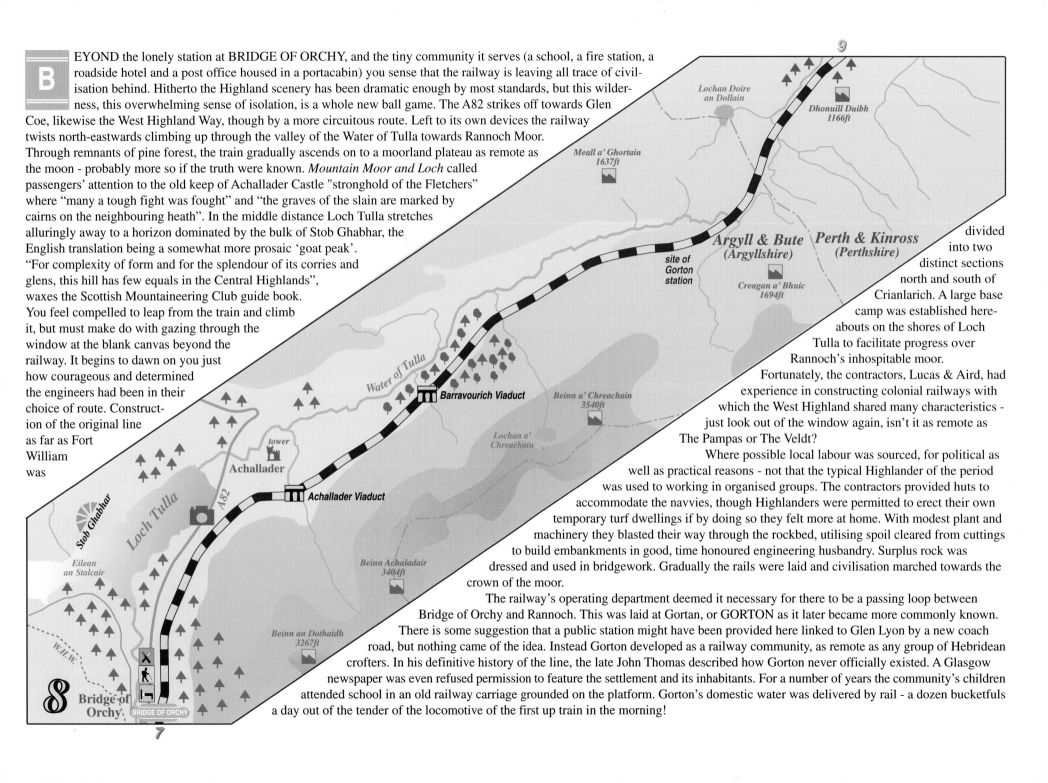

BEYOND the lonely station at BRIDGE OF ORCHY, and the tiny community it serves (a school, a fire station, a roadside hotel and a post office housed in a portacabin) you sense that the railway is leaving all trace of civilisation behind. Hitherto the Highland scenery has been dramatic enough by most standards, but this wilderness, this overwhelming sense of isolation, is a whole new ball game. The A82 strikes off towards Glen Coe, likewise the West Highland Way, though by a more circuitous route. Left to its own devices the railway twists north-eastwards climbing up through the valley of the Water of Tulla towards Rannoch Moor. Through remnants of pine forest, the train gradually ascends on to a moorland plateau as remote as the moon - probably more so if the truth were known. *Mountain Moor and Loch* called passengers' attention to the old keep of Achallader Castle "stronghold of the Fletchers" where "many a tough fight was fought" and "the graves of the slain are marked by cairns on the neighbouring heath". In the middle distance Loch Tulla stretches alluringly away to a horizon dominated by the bulk of Stob Ghabhar, the English translation being a somewhat more prosaic 'goat peak'. "For complexity of form and for the splendour of its corries and glens, this hill has few equals in the Central Highlands", waxes the Scottish Mountaineering Club guide book. You feel compelled to leap from the train and climb it, but must make do with gazing through the window at the blank canvas beyond the railway. It begins to dawn on you just how courageous and determined the engineers had been in their choice of route. Construction of the original line as far as Fort William was

divided into two distinct sections north and south of Crianlarich. A large base camp was established hereabouts on the shores of Loch Tulla to facilitate progress over Rannoch's inhospitable moor.

Fortunately, the contractors, Lucas & Aird, had experience in constructing colonial railways with which the West Highland shared many characteristics - just look out of the window again, isn't it as remote as The Pampas or The Veldt?

Where possible local labour was sourced, for political as well as practical reasons - not that the typical Highlander of the period was used to working in organised groups. The contractors provided huts to accommodate the navvies, though Highlanders were permitted to erect their own temporary turf dwellings if by doing so they felt more at home. With modest plant and machinery they blasted their way through the rockbed, utilising spoil cleared from cuttings to build embankments in good, time honoured engineering husbandry. Surplus rock was dressed and used in bridgework. Gradually the rails were laid and civilisation marched towards the crown of the moor.

The railway's operating department deemed it necessary for there to be a passing loop between Bridge of Orchy and Rannoch. This was laid at Gortan, or GORTON as it later became more commonly known. There is some suggestion that a public station might have been provided here linked to Glen Lyon by a new coach road, but nothing came of the idea. Instead Gorton developed as a railway community, as remote as any group of Hebridean crofters. In his definitive history of the line, the late John Thomas described how Gorton never officially existed. A Glasgow newspaper was even refused permission to feature the settlement and its inhabitants. For a number of years the community's children attended school in an old railway carriage grounded on the platform. Gorton's domestic water was delivered by rail - a dozen bucketfuls a day out of the tender of the locomotive of the first up train in the morning!

Map labels:

9

Lochan Doire an Dollain

Meall a' Ghortain 1637ft

Dhonuill Duibh 1166ft

Argyll & Bute *(Argyllshire)* **Perth & Kinross** *(Perthshire)*

site of Gorton station

Creagan a' Bhuic 1694ft

Water of Tulla

Barravourich Viaduct

Beinn a' Chreachain 3540ft

Lochan a' Chreachain

tower

Achallader

Achallader Viaduct

Stob Ghabhar

Loch Tulla

A82

Eilean an Stalcair

Beinn Achaladair 3404ft

Beinn an Dothaidh 3267ft

W.H.W.

8 Bridge of Orchy

BRIDGE OF ORCHY

7

ARGUABLY one of the most romantic railway destinations in the world, RANNOCH stands in splendid isolation: eighty-seven miles from Glasgow, thirty-five from Fort William, and a little matter of sixteen from Kinloch Rannoch, the nearest settlement of any size. Panic sets in as the train rumbles away into the distance: "What am I doing here, I must have been mad to get off the train." Then slowly but surely your confidence returns, stress evaporates and a sense of well-being takes over. There's no signal for your mobile phone, you cannot be got at, an invigorating feeling of optimism and potential manifests itself in your mind. However long you're here for, it is not time to be killed, but time to be treasured.

In reaching Rannoch from the south the train has traversed a unique landscape: half earth, half water, half real, half dream; a bog-strewn tableland absent-mindedly abandoned by retreating glaciers four hundred million years ago. Mostly, the line has been descending since Gorton, but once it has crossed the Abhainn Duibhe it climbs again. Look out on the western side of the line for signposted 'soldiers trenches' dug here by the Duke of Cumberland's men after the Forty-Five, both as an attempt at drainage and to provide useful employment for men who had a good deal of time on their hands.

The trenches are part of Rannoch folklore. So is the epic tale of January 1889 when a party of seven gentlemen connected with the nascent railway set out to walk across the moor southwards from Loch Treig to Inveroran on the banks of Loch Tulla to collect more knowledge of the lie of the land before construction commenced. Dressed, by all accounts, as if they were simply going shopping in Sauchiehall Street, the expedition, ill-judged at best in wintry conditions, might well have cost them their lives. The drama which subsequently unfolded would make great TV - young Scots playwrights take note - and you should at least turn to John Thomas's definitive *West Highland Railway* to learn the tale in fuller detail than we have space to flesh out here. Suffice to say that having missed an appointment with a local landowner at Rannoch and eschewed the chance of hospitality, the party plunged on across the moor as dusk fell, quickly becoming separated into ones and twos in the darkness. The oldest member of the group, a sexagenarian factor, collapsed. Two others, one of which was none other than Charles Forman the project's Chief Engineer, were overtaken by exhaustion and made what shelter they could behind a giant boulder. The two fittest men, James Bulloch, Forman's right hand man, and Robert McAlpine (who shouldn't need any introduction) continued, independently, southwards. Bulloch collided with a

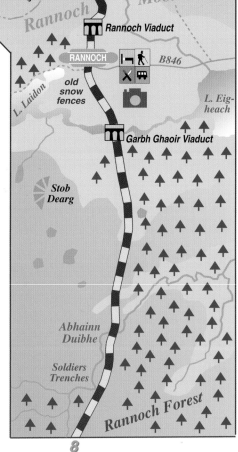

fence and lay stunned for four hours, but eventually reached Gortan and summoned aid for the rest. Nothing further was heard of McAlpine until the next day, when word came that he was safe in a cottage three miles down the Tulla Water. A terrible blizzard broke over the moor the next evening. Twenty-four hours earlier and the party would undoubtedly have perished.

Undaunted by this experience, Charles Forman proceeded to oversee building of the line, but three years after his misadventure construction had yet to gain any momentum across the moor. Subsidence was the major problem. The bog simply sucked in all the spoil deposited on it in an attempt to make a firm surface for the track to be laid on. Adopting principles pioneered by George Stephenson with the Liverpool & Manchester Railway where it crossed the unstable ground of Chat Moss, the line was 'floated' across the wettest sections of the moor on layers of turf and brushwood which the peaty soil effectively preserved as though it were vinegar and the brushwood onions. But as John Thomas succinctly put it: "the moor was swallowing money as well as material". With the promoters haemorrhaging capital, one director, J.A.Renton, dug deep into his own pocket to make good the shortfall. In gratitude, the navvies, who had feared for their jobs, manhandled a large boulder on to the platform at Rannoch station and carved out a profile of Renton on its durable face. It has stood the test of time, as good a monument as any man might hope for.

Rannoch station displays all the West Highland family traits, save that on this occasion access to the island platform from the outside world is by way of a footbridge as opposed to a subway. Though no railway staff are any longer employed on the premises, a tearoom and gift shop bring a reassuring sense of homeliness and activity. Keen railway eyes will spot the abandoned well of a former turntable and an old carriage used as a bothy by ScotRail's angling club. Somewhat surprisingly, given the tabletop terrain of the moor, the line's longest viaduct stands to the north of the station, carrying the line across a boggy depression which would perhaps have proved too thirsty to fill with any certainty. Its girders are supported on piers of granite conveniently extracted from the Cruach rock cutting less than a mile to the north where Britain's only snow shed was erected to protect the line from the wind's worst drifting.

I F you thought Rannoch was remote, see what you make of Corrour, the highest summit on the line. Initially, the station here was provided for railway workers and their families, and as a private facility for the nearby estate; though, unlike Gorton, in due course it found its way into the public timetables. Perhaps this was because it was to gain considerable custom from an unexpected source. In the early years of the twentieth century Kinlochleven, a village some ten miles west of Corrour as the crow flies, was invaded by navvies working on a hydro-electric scheme and aluminium works. Difficulty of access forced the men into the habit of using Corrour as a railhead, even though faced with a very long walk across dangerous peat bogs. By all accounts the Kinlochleven of those days closely resembled the Yukon in the gold rush. Lawlessness abounded, on one occasion, police combing the moor between the railway and Kinlochleven for a certain fugitive, missed their man but found the remains of three others. Grouse shooting and deer stalking provided other business for Corrour, and it officially opened to the public in 1934.

CORROUR station doesn't even run to the benefit of a metalled road, though a track leads eastwards along the shore of Loch Ossian to a youth hostel and a shooting lodge. "A fast-moving party" opines the SMC *Central Highlands District* guide book "can enjoy a day's hillwalking and a round trip from Corrour to Ben Alder between the morning and evening trains." Their enthusiasm is infectious - but you can always be inoculated. Corrour starred in the film *Trainspotting* adapted from Irving Welsh's novel of the same name. Not noted for its railway content, in spite of its title, the four main drug-crazed characters arrive here by train and make as if to climb Leum Uilleim, but turn back when they see how steep it is.

Corrour retains a loop but is not used by scheduled services. The former signalbox is used now as a bunkhouse, the station house a restaurant. One of the West Highland's best, though possibly apocryphal, stories concerns a brake van which became detached from its train following a rather excessively spirited acceleration away from the loop. The guard was sound asleep and immune to any jolting. As the train puffed away northwards, the brake van with comatose guard gently began to run back towards Rannoch. Strictly according to the rule book, the signalman at Rannoch should have turned the errant vehicle into a siding and derailed it, but in doing so he realised he would probably bring about the guard's death. Meanwhile

the brake van had built up enough momentum to carry it uphill to Gorton, where the signalman was equally loath to bring about a colleague's demise. Onward and downward it continued to Bridge of Orchy, miraculously staying on the track, and finally coming to a halt two miles away near the Horseshoe curve. The Bridge of Orchy stationmaster actually had to shake the guard awake, his van had freewheeled twenty-five miles.

Southbound trains face a daunting climb to Corrour, much of it at 1 in 67, steepening to 1 in 59 as they near the summit. The 1960 BBC documentary, *West Highland*, made by John Gray (who had been involved with the classic GPO film *Night Mail*) featured stirring scenes of Black Fives climbing this bank in its bleak bogland setting. Watching it now (on a Panamint Cinema video release) evokes nostalgia for the West Highland in the last years of steam, when the trains still ran to dining cars and observation carriages, when fish specials were still run from Mallaig, and when the children from wayside cottages could still flag down a train to take them to and from school.

Leaving Corrour on a clear day, you might catch a glimpse of Ben Nevis to the north-west. Loch Treig - the loch of desolation - rolls into view as the train runs downhill towards Glen Spean. An old drovers road passes under the railway, the authentic Road to the Isles of the old song, though don't be disappointed if Sir Harry Lauder isn't to be seen headed for the Cuillins with his cromack. Console yourself, the "tangle o' the Isles" can still be felt by humming that jaunty air and gazing through the window as the banks of the loch - whose depth varies according to the generating requirements of the aluminium smelter at Fort William - draw nearer as the railway descends the adjoining hillside. The mountains beyond the loch - Stob a' Choire Mheadhoin and Stob Coire Easain are popular not only with walkers but with skiers as well.

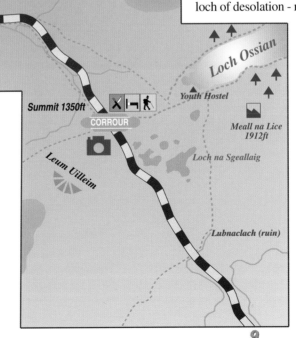

10

Stob a' Choire Mheadhoin 3610ft

Stob Coire Easain 3658ft

Stob Coire Sgriodain 3211ft

Loch Treig

Creagan a' Chase 2258ft

Creag Ghuanach 2035ft

Ben Nevis

Loch Ossian

Summit 1350ft

CORROUR

Youth Hostel

Meall na Lice 1912ft

Loch na Sgeallaig

Leum Uilleim

Lubnaclach (ruin)

A N almost cathartic change comes over the West Highland Railway as it descends from the bold, bare moorlands of Rannoch and Corrour and lands with a bump in the comparatively fertile valley of Glen Spean. At Tulloch a tight curve takes the line away from its northbound journeying and you head due west on the last lap into Fort William. Clinging to its cleft in the hillside, the line descends through Fersit Tunnel. You may have read elsewhere that, as built, the West Highland only had one tunnel. This one at Fersit dates from 1932 at which time a short deviation had to be built alongside Loch Treig which was having its water level raised by some thirty feet for the hydro-electric scheme connected with the aluminium plant at Fort William. While this work was being done, a temporary halt was opened at FERSIT for construction workers engaged on the project. With an eye well trained in spying out old trackbeds, you may just catch a glimpse of the original course of the line overgrown with silver birch below you.

TULLOCH station springs a surprise - there are *two* platforms! - though the architectural style plainly belongs to the West Highland 'Swiss chalet' family you have come to know so well since Garelochhead. Why change the status quo - something to do with the lie of the land along the valley floor, but if so why not provide a footbridge as at Rannoch and Corrour? It is a mystery which even West

levels in the glen as the glaciers retreated ten thousand years ago.

One 'road' which *was* man-made along the southern side of the glen belonged to the Lochaber Aluminium Railway, a three foot gauge line built in association with the aluminium plant at Fort William in the Nineteen-twenties. The line, known as the Upper Works Railway to distinguish it from another similarly-gauged section linking the smelter with a pier on Loch Linnhe, wound for nineteen miles along the mountainsides, reaching a summit of 1210 feet above sea level. Its initial purpose was to carry men and materials during construction of the scheme, but it was retained for maintenance access until the Seventies. Another great civil engineering undertaking was the construction of a pressure tunnel from Loch Treig to Fort William - 15 miles in length and big enough in diameter to carry a full size train inside.

Threading your way through the glen you come upon a pretty little church and its burial ground perched on the hillside at Achluachrach. It's a Catholic church and there's a good story concerning a Protestant packman, inadvertently buried here, whose spirit caused such a commotion at night that the graveyard had to be reconsecrated.

The railway reaches a dramatic narrowing at Monessie Gorge. *Mountain Moor & Loch* waxed typically lyrical at this point: "No spectacle on the line more forcibly impresses the memory ... the steep black rocks, the dark green foliage at the waters edge, and the white torrent boiling down the rugged bed in a mad delirious ferment ... proud, turbulent and untameable." Sadly, the Spean is rarely so boisterous nowadays on account of water extraction from Loch Laggan, further upstream.

Parallel Roads are even more strongly defined in Glen Roy - those of a geological bent are urged to detrain at ROY BRIDGE and explore. The station has lost its loop and a timber hut provides the only trace of hospitality. Up on a neighbouring hillside the last of Scotland's clan battles (other than the latest Old Firm game) was fought in 1689.

Highland experts, such as Dr John McGregor of the Open University and John Barnes of Glenfinnan Station Museum, remain puzzled by. Whatever the logic, Tulloch was also notable in being a preferred point for engines to fill their tenders to the brim with water. Apparently the water rates at Fort William were formidably high! Nowadays a popular bunkhouse occupies the main station building on the up platform, the loop is still in use and there's a kick-back siding for engineering plant.

The intimate woodlands of Glen Spean come as great contrast to moorland memories retained from Rannoch. The River Spean races along with you, creaming over rocks into pewter coloured pools. The prominent terraces on the neighbouring hillsides are "parallel roads", not some typically over ambitious Ministry of Transport initiative, but a phenomenon which puzzled geographers until their origin was satisfactorily explained by a Swiss glaciologist in the mid nineteenth century. Prior to that there had been some belief that the terraces were man-made, whereas, in reality, there were formed by diminishing water

PRESSED to list the most ill-conceived and impecunious railways ever built, most informed sources would sooner rather than later bring up the name of the Invergarry & Fort Augustus Railway. Little trace remains of its junction with the West Highland at SPEAN BRIDGE, but it was a double track turnout, ambitiously built for high speed running, as if the railway's local promoters had more in mind than a twenty-four mile branchline. Of course they did, they wanted to run through the Great Glen to Inverness in an echo of the Glasgow & North Western scheme of 1880. That they also failed - spectacularly! - is a melancholy comment on British politics and business rivalry: the only people who ever made a profit from all of Scotland's unbuilt railways were those of the legal profession; in the wake of privatisation, nothing much has changed.

Much of the Spean Bridge - Fort Augustus line's capital outlay came from the deep pockets of the Englishman who'd made his fortune brewing Bass. Unfortunately, so much was spent on building the line that the company couldn't afford any motive power or rolling stock. In turn, the Highland and North British were contracted to work the line, but in neither case was income anywhere near the operating expense. Eight years after it was opened, services ceased. Ironically, the railway company proceeded to make more money by sacking most of their staff, letting their homes and selling crops grown on the line's embankments, than by operating trains.

In 1912 there was a General Election and the fate of the line became something of a local issue. The North British Railway offered to buy it, only to be outbid by a scrap merchant. The local council made up the difference after discovering that with no trains running it was costing them more in upkeep of the roads. Trains recommenced running in 1914: passenger services somehow survived until 1933; the odd coal train, miraculously, until 1946.

Beneath the great bulk of Ben Nevis, your train jogs down into Fort William. Fidgeting fellow passengers gather their possessions, the sense of a journey accomplished is almost palpable. Fort William manifests itself in the shape of a golf course; a distillery, which once relied heavily on rail; and an aluminium works, which still does. The manufacture of aluminium is centred on Lochaber because of the availability of cheap hydro-electric power. The Lochaber Smelter opened in 1929 and has relied on rail transport ever since. Alumina (a derivative of bauxite) is brought by ship from Eire to North Blyth on the Northumberland coast where Alcan have another plant. Eighty thousand tonnes of alumina is conveyed in Alcan's own tank wagons by EWS to Fort William annually. Aluminium is manufactured by passing an electrical current through this raw material. Every two tonnes of alumina yield one tonne of aluminium ingots. These ingots are conveyed by Freightliner train to a rolling mill at Rogerstone in South Wales. Rail freight traffic to and from the works has, over the years, protected the West Highland line from threats of closure. The remains of Old Inverlochy Castle overlook the line, a 13th century stronghold last seriously fought over in 1645 when an army of clansmen lead by the Marquis of Argyll failed in their attempt to capture the castle from Royalist forces.

Tradition fleetingly re-invents itself at Fort William Junction where the tracks come under the control of a manual signal box and semaphore signalling. Between the Glasgow and Mallaig lines, a fan-like spread of sidings provides stabling facilities for First Engineering and EWS. Here too is a recently reinstated turntable, acquired after much fund-raising, from Marylebone, London, and installed to permit the turning of steam locomotives used on the summer *Jacobite* service to and from Mallaig.

On their way into Fort William the railway builders demolished the town's 17th century fortifications and replaced them with an engine shed. Nothing was sacred, the railway station insinuated itself between the town and Loch Linnhe. There it remained, spoiling the view, until 1975, when a modern replacement was provided. Railway purists might miss the old station's lochside setting, but most of 'The Fort's' inhabitants and visitors prefer the new way of things, even if a new dual carriageway ring road has to be crossed to reach the pier where the little passenger ferry waits for Camusnagaul, an intriguing coda to your journey perhaps and an opportunity, weather permitting, to see Ben Nevis at its best.

B8004

crse of Fort Augustus rly

Meall nan Luath 1387ft

Commando Memorial

Spean Bridge

A82

R. Spean

A86

SPEAN BRIDGE

Inverroy

Spean Viaduct

11

golf course

General Wade's Military Road

A82

Forest Walks

R. Lundy

Torlundy

13

R. Lochy

A830

distillery

golf course   course of old rly

Rubha Dearg

Ben Nevis

An Carol

Lochy Viaduct

Inverlochy Castle

rly depot

Aluminium Works

oil depot

Fort William Junction

passenger ferry

Loch Linnhe

FORT WILLIAM

pier

Town Centre

Fort William

12

A861

R. Nevis

Station to Station

West Highland stations have considerable charm and character, notably the Swiss chalet style of the original West Highland Railway. Happily many are finding new uses as bunkhouses and restaurants.

Main picture: Bridge of Orchy in the gloaming.
Left inset: Coupling up at Crianlarich.
Right inset: Level crossing, Morar.
Opposite clockwise from top left: Britain's westernmost station at Arisaig, with the Sgurr of Eigg jutting over the horizon. A cold wait for the first train of the day at Tulloch. Ironwork detail at Ardlui. Old signalling cabin interior, Bridge of Orchy. The imposing station at Dalmally on the Oban line. Interior of the fascinating Station Museum at Glenfinnan. The lonely station at Corrour, the power for its lights generated by wind turbine.
Centre: Morning mists rise over Arrochar & Tarbet.

Steam Dreams

James Shuttleworth

Steam trains are a feature of the Fort William to Mallaig route in the summer months when the West Coast Railway Company's *Jacobite* is in operation. At other times charters and excursions bring the sights and sounds of working steam to the West Highland Lines.

This page: Standard Class 4MT 75014 *Braveheart* treads cautiously over the swing-bridge at Banavie with *The Jacobite* while Ben Nevis forms a cloudy backdrop.

Opposite page, top left: Edward Thompson's mixed traffic B1 Class were regular performers on the West Highland, though rare over the Mallaig Extension. 1264 is seen here in LNER apple green.

Top right : The B1, now in British Railways black and renumbered 61264, on a photographers' charter at Tulloch station. This locomotive is earmarked to be a regular on *The Jacobite* in 2001.

Lower left: A Stanier 8F crosses Lochy Viaduct near Fort William.

Lower right: 75014 again, this time Mallaig bound on Loch nan Uamh Viaduct.

A snowy day on Rannoch Moor

A blanket of snow on Rannoch Moor and deer down from the hill to feed.
This page: A northbound EWS 'Enterprise' container train crosses Rannoch Viaduct with a RETB fitted General Motors Class 66 in charge.
Opposite main picture: Alert deer watch the train as it continues across the frozen wastes towards Corrour.
Left inset: A Class 156 ScotRail Sprinter leaves Rannoch station for Glasgow.
Right inset: The West Highland 'Swiss chalet' architecture seems appropriate as it frames Freightliner's southbound Alcan aluminium ingots train hauled by a Class 37 diesel on hire from EPS.

Trainspotting

37418 EW&S

East Lancashire Railways

Peter J. Robinson

Diesels have character too! Here are some of the designs regularly seen on the West Highland Lines.

Opposite page: The Caledonian Sleeper climbs away from Bridge of Orchy. ScotRail lease Class 37/4s from EWS to provide both motive power and electrical train heating.

Top left: The Canadian built, General Motors Class 66 is EWS's standard freight locomotive now. Here one shunts timber wagons in the yard at Crianlarich while, somewhat unusually, a Strathclyde cream and red coloured Class 156 Sprinter forms a West Highland service train.

Lower left: ScotRail's standard service train for the West Highland Lines is the Class 156 Sprinter unit built in Birmingham by Metro-Cammell in the late 1980s. Looking attractive in its ScotRail colours of purple, green and orange, this one has just arrived at Oban station.

Lower right: A Fragonset owned Class 31 leaves Mallaig with an excursion train for Fort William. Though an even more elderly design than the English Electric Class 37, the Brush built Class 31s could conceivably, if suitably refurbished, be leased by ScotRail to haul the sleeper service in future.

Dennis Hardley

Phil Connell

FORT WILLIAM & MALLAIG

LNER **WESTERN HIGHLANDS** LMS
IT'S QUICKER BY RAIL
FULL INFORMATION FROM LNER AND LMS OFFICES AND AGENCIES

Loch Eilt

The Jacobite, Glenfinnan

MORE frivolous than their Glasgow counterparts, Fort William-Mallaig trains feature on many a tourist itinerary. Coachloads descend on the train, bristling with cameras, cling-wrapped picnics and banal remarks; Robert Louis Stevenson's "canting dilettanti" personified. Unused to trains, they lack the sang-froid of the seasoned traveller. But, like you, they're here to savour one of the world's great railway journeys, so live and let live!

There's always something disconcerting when a train reverses out the way it's come in. Look out for the oil depot which should soon be receiving supplies by rail again following the upgrading of the rail terminal at Grangemouth. The adjoining bridge used to carry a narrow gauge line from the smelter to a quay on Loch Linnhe. At Fort William Junction the Mallaig line veers away in a north-westerly direction, crossing the River Lochy on a photogenic viaduct of iron girders supported by battlemented stone columns; uncharacteristic ornamentation said to be in homage to the neighbouring ruin of Inverlochy Castle.

Up until the Second World War a spur led to a little station called Banavie Pier on the banks of the Caledonian Canal. Excursionists used this short branch to connect with pleasure cruises on the canal, and there was a certain amount of goods transhipped as well, by dint

more reliable than it had been when first mooted in the 18th century. Here, at the western end of the canal, there were problems of access and employment. A brewery was built at Corpach in an attempt to 'induce the workmen to relinquish the pernicious habit of drinking whisky.' Telford remarked: "Misunderstandings and interruptions must be expected amongst a people just emerging from barbarism."

Passing the Arjo Wiggins paper mill which brings welcome rail freight business (china clay in, finished rolls of paper out) the line, accompanied by the A830 - or, more romantically, the Road to the Isles - runs in hauntingly beautiful mode along Loch Eil. Across the water, pockets of woodland recede as bare shoulders of moorland rise to Stob Coire a' Chearcaill - 2525ft. Through boles of silver birch you can look back, south-eastwards, to Ben Nevis (4406ft), often shrouded in cloud in otherwise fine weather, though leaving you in no doubt as to the girth, bearing and stature of Britain's highest mountain.

LOCH EIL OUTWARD BOUND is a simple wooden platform provided for those alighting for the adjacent adventure centre whose boathouses cluster attractively by the water's edge. Trains call at LOCHEILSIDE the next station, three or four miles along the loch, by request only. Workshops and a pier were erected here when the Extension was being built.

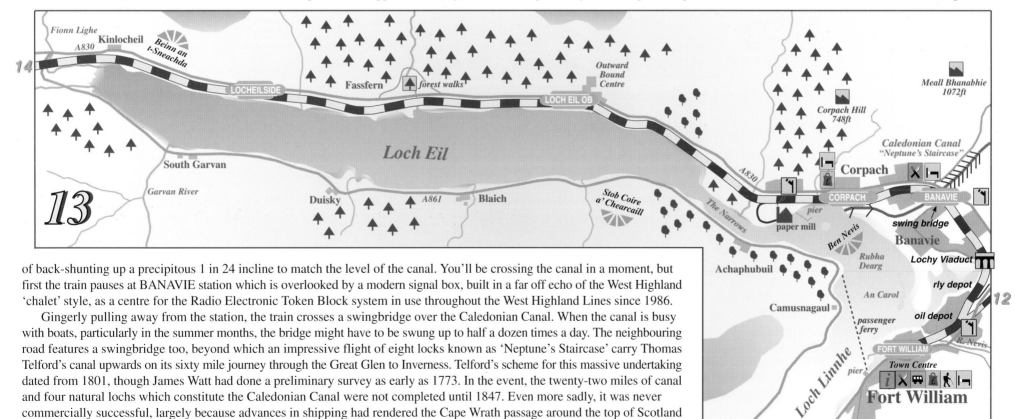

of back-shunting up a precipitous 1 in 24 incline to match the level of the canal. You'll be crossing the canal in a moment, but first the train pauses at BANAVIE station which is overlooked by a modern signal box, built in a far off echo of the West Highland 'chalet' style, as a centre for the Radio Electronic Token Block system in use throughout the West Highland Lines since 1986.

Gingerly pulling away from the station, the train crosses a swingbridge over the Caledonian Canal. When the canal is busy with boats, particularly in the summer months, the bridge might have to be swung up to half a dozen times a day. The neighbouring road features a swingbridge too, beyond which an impressive flight of eight locks known as 'Neptune's Staircase' carry Thomas Telford's canal upwards on its sixty mile journey through the Great Glen to Inverness. Telford's scheme for this massive undertaking dated from 1801, though James Watt had done a preliminary survey as early as 1773. In the event, the twenty-two miles of canal and four natural lochs which constitute the Caledonian Canal were not completed until 1847. Even more sadly, it was never commercially successful, largely because advances in shipping had rendered the Cape Wrath passage around the top of Scotland

IT'S possible to become blasé in the face of such breathtaking beauty. Wherever your gaze lingers there is something to catch your eye as the train climbs at 1 in 50 up to Glenfinnan. Is there a more spellbinding railway setting in the British Isles? Certainly Glenfinnan Viaduct has the poise to keep heady company with the likes of Ribblehead, Knucklas, St Germans and any other railway bridge you care to mention. The astonishing thing, of course, is that Glenfinnan Viaduct is built of concrete, that much maligned material, so uncompromisingly ugly in the wrong hands, but here almost organic in its harmony with the landscape. Statistics are almost irrelevant, but you might like to know that the viaduct is 416 yards long, set on a twelve chain curve, and that the tallest of its 21 arches is a hundred feet above the ground. It was designed by the Glasgow engineering

lost its characteristic station buildings and signal box had a young Englishman called John Barnes not stepped in to preserve a typical example of railway architecture on a line he'd come to know and love as a teenager. The resulting Station Museum is well worth missing the train for, though you cannot help but feel a tinge of sadness that most of its fascinating exhibits have been modernised out of everyday railway use. Besides his museum, John has also found time to refurbish two old railway carriages for use as a cafe and sleeping car respectively; the latter carrying on a tradition of camping coach provision at this location which dates back to the 1930s. Indeed, all West Highland stations with the exception of Corrour, Lochailort and

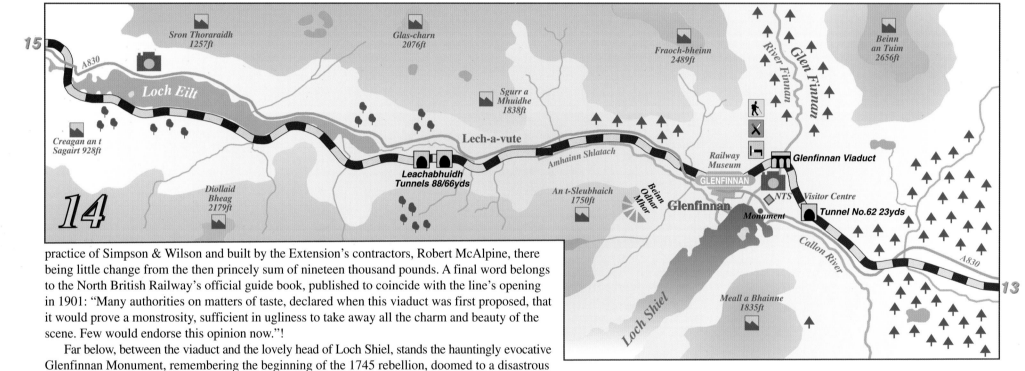

practice of Simpson & Wilson and built by the Extension's contractors, Robert McAlpine, there being little change from the then princely sum of nineteen thousand pounds. A final word belongs to the North British Railway's official guide book, published to coincide with the line's opening in 1901: "Many authorities on matters of taste, declared when this viaduct was first proposed, that it would prove a monstrosity, sufficient in ugliness to take away all the charm and beauty of the scene. Few would endorse this opinion now."!

Far below, between the viaduct and the lovely head of Loch Shiel, stands the hauntingly evocative Glenfinnan Monument, remembering the beginning of the 1745 rebellion, doomed to a disastrous end at Culloden. The figure on top of the tower is not, as is sometimes thought, Bonnie Prince Charlie himself, but a symbolic Highland chieftain sculpted by one John Greenshields, a friend of Sir Walter Scott. The monument itself was built by Alexander Macdonald in 1815, something of a rake, who died at the age of 28 owing the equivalent of some four million pounds by today's standards. We should forgive him his extravagances, the monument is worth every penny saved by more fiscally judicious men.

The railway rounds on GLENFINNAN station through a rocky cutting that was the source of much material used in the construction of the viaduct; no wonder it looks as though it has literally grown out of the landscape. When radio signalling reached Mallaig, Glenfinnan might well have

Beasdale featured Camping Coaches in LNER days, typically available at a rental of £3 per week!

Beyond Glenfinnan the train continues to climb towards the watershed. If you're lucky enough to be on *The Jacobite,* the glorious sound of a steam engine working hard will be ricochetting around the rocky hills. There was once a privately owned halt at Lech-a-vute. Negotiating two short tunnels called Leachabhuidh, the line then descends at 1 in 48 to run along the shores of the freshwater Loch Eilt for three or four miles of beguiling loveliness. On an islet at the western end of the loch grow pine trees left behind by the Great Caledonian Forest.

15

Back of Keppoch

ARISAIG

Arisaig

Loch nan Ceall

Torr Mor
268ft

Loch
nan
Eala

Loch Dubh

A830

Arisaig
House

Prince
Charlie's
Cave

Borrodale Viaduct
Borrodale Tunnel 350yrds

BEASDALE

Beasdale Tunnels 192/154yrds

Loch nan Uamh Tunnels 66/99yrds

Loch na Creige Duibhe

Loch Mama

Creag Bhan
1675ft

Loch nan Uamh

Prince's
Cairn

Loch nanUamh or Gleann Mama Viaduct

Loch Beag

Arnabol Viaduct

Loch Dubh

**Polnish Tunnels
38/44yrds**

Our Lady of the Braes

LOCHAILORT

A830
memorial

14

**Lochailort Tunnel
176yrds**

Lochan a
Ghobhainn

Loch Doir a Ghearrain

Eilean Dubh

Loch Ailort

A861

Inverailort

WHEN the Mallaig Extension was being built, the largest work camp was established at Lochailort. Two thousand navvies at its busiest: Irish, Highland and Lowland Scots (almost separate races), and even Scandinavians, who must have felt at home in such a landscape. To echo Napoleon, navvies, like armies, march on their stomachs. McAlpines appreciated this and contracted a high class firm of Glasgow merchants to provision their workforce. Nevertheless, labour was hard to keep hold of and the perennial problem of recruitment, added to the intractable nature of the indigenous rock - just look out of the window! - caused the construction schedule repeatedly to slip.

LOCHAILORT station is another of the Extension's request stops; though once it was a proper station with buildings and a passing loop where mail was unloaded for the Moidart peninsular. Hereabouts, the original concept of a line reaching out to embrace the fishing trade at Roshven would have veered southwards. Luckily, local opposition and political meddling forced the railway's promoters into a rethink, otherwise we would never have had the magnificent last lap of the line to enjoy.

Twisting and climbing in and out of tunnels, the railway skirts Loch Ailort, scene of the initial Commando training programme instigated by Winston Churchill in 1942, the locality west of Fort William being considered 'out of bounds' to unauthorised civilians during the Second World War. One of the Extension's best known landmarks is the isolated church of Our Lady of the Braes an incongruously whitewashed building which features on many a postcard. It was used in Bill Forsyth's film *Local Hero* for the scene where the villagers vote on their willingness to sell their beautiful locality to an oil company. Sadly the church, consecrated in 1870, has had no regular services since 1964, and has recently been purchased for conversion to a private dwelling.

Switchbacking downhill the line skirts Loch Dubh which the railway builders dammed to provide power for a turbine used to drive the rock drills engaged in clearing a course for the Extension. The idea for a turbine had come to Malcolm McAlpine - 'Concrete Bob's' younger son - after a visit to the dentist in Helensburgh! John Thomas tells the tale more fully in his *West Highland Railway*, where he also relates the harrowing story of Malcolm's serious injury in a cutting explosion. The camp doctor at Lochailort reported that the nineteen year old had multiple fractures and serious internal injuries and that he was unlikely to live. A telegram was sent to this effect to Sir Robert McAlpine in Glasgow who immediately got in touch with one of the city's most distinguished surgeons. A specially hired train took them through the night to Fort William, from where they travelled for seven hours by horse and cart to Lochailort. In the barely equipped camp hospital, the surgeon performed a major operation and subsequently sat by his patient for four days. Eventually it was decided that only hope of saving the young man's life was to get him down to Glasgow, but he could not be taken to Fort William by road because the jolting would have killed him. So he was carried overland

by stretcher and rowed across lochs and in time came to Banavie where a special train was waiting to take him to Glasgow. Such care was well rewarded, he lived to a ripe old age!

Glenfinnan Viaduct receives most of the plaudits, but some connoisseurs of the Extension feel that Loch nan Uamh Viaduct is the pick of the line's viaducts. Less spectacular, but more gorgeous in its coastal setting, it offers Mallaig-bound travellers their first view of the luxuriant, Gulf Stream washed shores of the Atlantic Ocean. Legend has it that a horse and cart fell into the viaduct's central abutment as it was being built and, being too difficult to recover, were abandoned therein for eternity.

Roadside, well below the railway, a cairn on the rocky shoreline of Loch nan Uamh marks the point from which Bonnie Prince Charlie left Scotland for France after his defeat at Culloden. BEASDALE was initially a private station for the owner of Arisaig House. Borrodale Viaduct has a massive span of 127ft 6ins. Carriage wheels squealing in protest at the tight radius of the curves, Britain's westernmost railway station, ARISAIG, is reached.

TANTALISINGLY the line twists inland, as if stage-managing the final coastal run into Mallaig for maximum effect. To the west the land lies flat providing a semblance of fertile farmland; eastwards it rises sharply up to the 1,286ft summit of Sgurr an Albanaich.

Swinging northwards in a determined attempt to reach Mallaig, astonishing views seaward are apt to be accompanied by audible gasps in a welter of tongues from the tourists among your fellow passengers. The locals keep their heads down in newspapers - oblivious to the beauty.

Running downhill, the train picks up speed as if sensing the finishing line, the bogies beating out a not unfunky rhythm on the tracks. A boggy interlude precedes the penultimate station at Morar, a small community famed for the whiteness of its sands, the brevity of its eponymous river and the proximity of the deepest (1,017ft at its maximum) expanse of freshwater (Loch Morar) in Britain. The loch is reputed to be home to a monster even shyer than Nessie, but has thankfully been spared all the trappings of tourism.

A cross crowns a rocky bluff overlooking the line. It commemorates "a very successful mission" by the Redemptorist Fathers hereabouts on the 21st July 1889. The present cross of iron dates from 1965, the original having been renewed on several occasions, testimony to the force of Atlantic gales, no doubt, rather than any lack of religious conviction.

The Road to the Isles is nearing the end of its journey too, but it has had money spent on it, and now by-passes Morar. Perhaps the once picturesque petrol station by the level crossing is a victim of the detour, and one casually wonders if the hotel has suffered a loss of trade as well. Once it was known as the Station Hotel and here, between 1928 and 1940 the composer Arnold Bax would stay each winter, in search of peace and quiet and inspiration for his music. His preferred room (No.11) overlooked a majestic view across the white-sanded bay to Eigg and Rhum, and the Celt in Bax was suitably inspired by the landscape, if not the cold. Those already beguiled by the music of this scandalously neglected British composer will very likely feel compelled to alight at Morar and pay homage to the scenes of his muse. A walk across the sands whilst humming the memorable

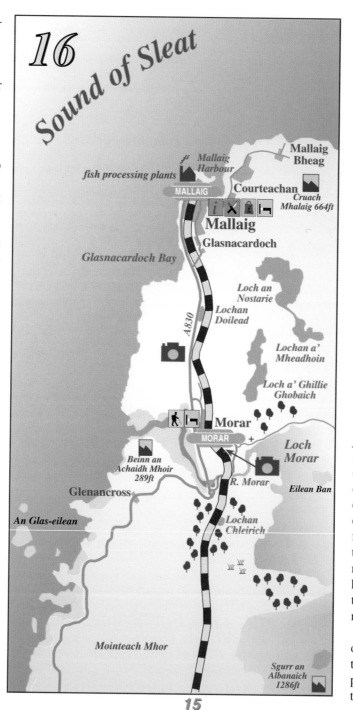

16 **Sound of Sleat**

epilogue from the Third Symphony can be thoroughly recommended.

The cinema also has reason to be grateful to Morar, for as at Polnish, encountered earlier in the journey, scenes from Bill Forsyth's quirky comedy *Local Hero* were filmed in the sand dunes in and around the estuary; memorably the scene where Burt Lancaster is invited into the hovel which provides a home for the beachcomber Fulton McKay.

Music, literature, films, the West Highland has them all - and views to die for too! Briefly, though, these become uncharacteristically restricted as the train faces a short climb before commencing its descent into Mallaig. So, passing between the modest summits of Bourblach and Beoraidbeg hills and skirting the reed-fringed bank of Lochan Doilead, views are restricted until Glasnacardoch Bay is reached and the full panorama of the Sound of Sleat is revealed as a fitting climax to the run from Fort William. There, at last, are those "far Coolins" that have been "puttin love" on us, all along this 'railway to the isles'. And there also, in closer detail than we have yet seen them, are Eigg and Rhum broadsides on, adding yet more intoxication to the scene as you traverse the last mile into Mallaig itself.

Seaside termini have always held a special place in the hearts of railway enthusiasts; especially the modelling fraternity. Perhaps it's the simplicity of pointwork that appeals, the sheer scenic potential, or the sense of a long journey meaningfully and fulfillingly ended. Short trains and glamorous motive power play their part, or at least did in the days before the ubiquitous Sprinter. Archive photographs depict a Mallaig railhead close to the ideal, attractively canopied and buttressed against the prevailing gales; with a one-road engine shed, a steam crane for coaling and sidings for the fish traffic. Modernisation and rationalisation have taken their inevitable toll, though at least the run-round loop remains for *The Jacobite* steamers and other locomotive hauled excursions, whilst there are firm plans to reinstate a turntable to provide a necessary counterpart to the one recently installed at Fort William.

Meanwhile here you are at journey's end. Perhaps one of the islands beckons, or simply a trip to see the seals, or the taste of fish & chips *al fresco* on the quay. However you pass the time, pass it fruitfully, you've just enjoyed one of the world's 'great' railway journeys - make the memory last.

CRIANLARICH & OBAN

LOCH ETIVE
WESTERN HIGHLANDS
ON THE ROUTE OF THE GLENCOE, GLEN ETIVE
AND LOCH ETIVE CIRCULAR TOUR

BRITISH RAILWAYS

BRITISH RAILWAYS

Connel Ferry

Dennis Hardley

Royal Scotsman, Tyndrum Lower

Peter J. Robinson

NOWADAYS, of course, the Oban and Fort William routes are seamlessly integrated under the West Highland banner. Railtrack own the permanent way and ScotRail provide the passenger services. No good reason, then, why there should be any difference in character or atmosphere. And yet there remains an almost palpable sense that, from Crianlarich westwards to the sea, you are travelling over a quite *different* railway; a railway, perhaps, more at ease with its surroundings, a railway built with a bigger budget! You have to go back almost forty years to find the lines being operated independently out of Glasgow's Buchanan Street and Queen Street stations, and even further, prior to the 1948 Nationalisation of the railway system, to the era of the London Midland Scottish and London & North Eastern railway companies, to discover the source of these character traits. It wasn't just a matter of rolling stock and architecture, more an unquantifiable sense of company pride, and even to this day there is good natured rivalry and banter between Oban and Fort William based railway staff.

The two routes' scenery is in contrast as well. Where the West Highland goes boldly up and over the hills to Rannoch, the Oban line sets a more demure course, threading its way through Glen Lochy in altogether more genteel circumstances. You pick up this thread west of the summit at Tyndrum (Map 7) as the line falls past Lochan na Bi in close company with the A85, both transport infrastructures hemmed in by ranks of conifer plantations - significantly, the glen was virtually bereft of trees when the railway was built in 1877. Beyond the trees the glen's flanks rise precipitously to sizeable summits, culminating, to the south, with the

Succoth Viaduct was scene of a charming ceremony on its completion in November 1876. That reliable chronicler of Scottish railway history, the late John Thomas, described the occasion with typically stylish prose in his book *The Callander & Oban Railway*. Though it was a raw afternoon, a party of ladies and gentlemen journeyed up the line in a contractor's wagon to witness the bridgebuilder's wife set the keystone. "In this bizarre and chilly setting the whisky flowed, the bagpipes skirled, and the guests danced until the gathering darkness drove them back to their train".

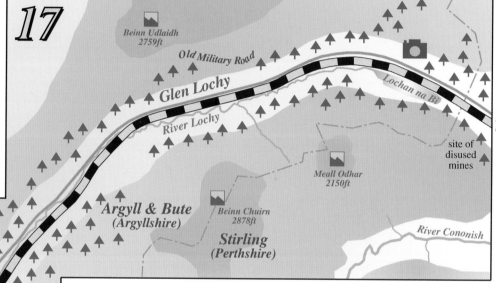

magnificence of Ben Lui, 3708ft high and usually snow-capped well into early summer.

It's downhill all the way to Dalmally, in terms of gradient that is, certainly not scenically, with the River Lochy providing you with entertaining company, first to the left and then to the right of the Oban-bound train. In busier days there was a crossing loop approximately halfway between Tyndrum and Dalmally, but it didn't survive the Nineteen-sixties; since then the frequency of passenger trains on the Oban line has been halved whilst, currently, only the timber traffic from Taynuilt provides the line with any freight, though there are indications that oil traffic may return before too long.

When line opened through to Dalmally on May day 1877, horse-drawn coaches connected with the trains to provide passengers with a link to Oban. Other enterprising coach operators ran to meet with MacBrayne's steamers on Loch Fyne. Dual-platformed and still boasting a passing-loop, the station at DALMALLY retains a sizeable building, an imposing station house and a timber signal cabin; all sadly empty (though it may soon become another bunkhouse) a far cry from the days when, as recalled in the village's local history booklet: "the railway showed a warm, human face to the public - dropping your parcels off at the farm gate or bringing you home from a ceilidh on the 3am mail!" The local cattle mart brought regular business to the goodsyard and at one time there was even an engine shed, perhaps retained (after the line had been extended to Oban) with a view towards Dalmally becoming the junction for a branchline to Inveraray. Two world wars brought increased traffic to the station. In the first one it was a case of men leaving the glen - many of them for the first time (and the last), in the second, large numbers of Allied troops arrived in Dalmally by rail to train for D-Day. Incidentally, keep an eye out on the down platform for a curious heron-shaped fountain made of Cruachan granite.

BETWEEN Dalmally and Taynuilt there is barely a dull moment as the railway firstly runs picturesquely alongside Loch Awe then dramatically negotiates the Pass of Brander, famous for its 'stone' signals which protect the line from avalanches. Building of the final twenty-four miles of railway between Dalmally and Oban commenced in 1878. The year's hiatus following completion of the line to Dalmally had been spent raising funds for the last lap to the sea! It was no easy task laying a railway through this rugged landscape. Floods and frosts played havoc with the building schedule. A ship bringing rails from Workington in Westmorland foundered on rocks in Loch Etive and was deemed a total wreck, though some of the rails were salvaged.

Today's scenic train ride is the result of Victorian determination and ingenuity.

Gradients done with for the time being, the railway emerges from woodland and crosses Orchy Viaduct at the head of Loch Awe. Suddenly there is a scintillating view of the romantically ruined Kilchurn Castle. Immediately you want to leave the train and somehow reach that magical setting. And you can! From the delightful lochside station of LOCH AWE, a steam launch runs to the

castle precincts throughout the summer months. Re-opened in 1985, after an absence from the timetable of twenty years, Loch Awe station has lost all its buildings (which archive photographs depict as once having had much charm) but an old carriage serves as a welcome cafe while you wait for your boat to come in. High above the station a massive Scottish baronial style hotel was built to profit from the many holiday-makers brought in to the area with the advent of the railway. At one time the platform and the hotel were connected by the latest thing in electric lifts. In 1924 Mary Pickford, Douglas Fairbanks and Ivor Novello stayed in the hotel. Four years later it was the turn of American tennis champions Helen Wills and Bill Tilden to enjoy their breakfast porridge in such a stimulating

setting. From sidings at Loch Awe station, coal was once transhipped into cargo vessels for distribution to settlements along the loch's twenty-three mile length. In return they would bring timber and agricultural produce for despatch by rail to other parts of Scotland.

Now follows a charming interlude as the line affectionately hugs the north shoreline of Loch Awe. A fish farm out in the middle of the loch catches your eye. On level track the train picks up speed, but you're in no hurry to lose such ravishing views. All too soon, however, the railway starts climbing, twisting in a north-westerly direction to thread its way through the Pass of Brander. Under the towering ramparts of Ben Cruachan the line is forced alongside the cantilevered road on to a slender ledge as the loch narrows into the River Awe. The resultant ravine is so steep that you are forced to crane your neck to see the sky. A halt was opened at FALLS OF CRUACHAN for visitors to the nearby waterfall in 1893. Nowadays the station only appears in the summer timetable as a request halt for people heading to the Cruachan Power Station Visitor Centre. Ben Cruachan (3689ft) is known as the 'hollow mountain' because the hydro-electric scheme utilises hollowed out caverns within the hillside to house its machinery. Railfans might recognise the mountain as inspiration for a name given to one of the Class 37 diesel locomotives long-associated with the West Highland lines.

In August, 1881 a local train, moving slowly through the Pass of Brander, was hit by a falling boulder. It had been an accident waiting to happen. In response, the line's indefatigable manager, John Anderson, devised a series of tripwires which would activate semaphore warning signals in the event of further rockfalls. The system remains in use to this day, having stood the test of time, being quaintly known as 'Anderson's Piano' on account of the humming sound made by the wind in the wires.

Beyond the Pass of Brander the line drops again, crosses the river on a high viaduct and runs through conifer plantations to reach TAYNUILT station. Bare platforms are all that remain of an ambitious plan to create a railway museum here before a tragic fire rendered the remains suitable only for demolition. Happily the sidings remain used by timber traffic.

18

Bonawe
Loch Etive
jetty
Brochroy
Inverawe Ho. Country Park
A85
9
TAYNUILT
Nant Viaduct
Taynuilt
River Nant
B845
Awe Viaduct
Bridge of Awe
River Awe
'stone' signals
Pass of Brander
Lochan na Cuaig
Ben Cruachan
Meall Cuanail 3004ft
Cruachan Reservoir
Beinn a' Bhuiridh 2941ft
Falls of Cruachan
FALLS OF CRUACHAN
'stone' signals
Power Station Visitor Centre
Innis Chonain
Lochawe
LOCH AWE
Loch Awe
A85
Orchy Viaduct
Stronmilchan
River Strae
B8077
Kilchurn Castle
A819
17

FOUR hundred men were employed on building the last stage of the Callander & Oban railway, and they were, according to a local newspaper: "the lowest type of men, capable of committing any evil action". Be that as it may, the line they built lives on after them as testimony to their hard work if not their hard drinking. Ideally, the railway's promoters would have preferred to approach Oban by way of the coast through Dunstaffnage and Ganavan, but obdurate landowners forced them to go inland and face a steep climb to Glencruitten summit, before descending to reach the town from the south.

Between Taynuilt and Connel Ferry the route lay largely along the southern shore of Loch Etive. At Ach-na-Cloich a small station was opened to serve an adjoining steamer pier. Little remains of this activity save for a ruined timber building, but early in the 20th century there was even a "Loch Etive Boat Train" which would steam proudly up from Oban as part of a circular tour involving road, rail and water transport. Now the quiet little bay is home to a shellfish farm and little else.

Playing hide and seek with the shoreline, wheels squealing on the tight curves, the train slows for CONNEL FERRY. There are glimpses of the impressive cantilever bridge built originally to carry the Ballachulish branch across the Falls of Lora. The line's closure in 1966 was predictable in an era blind to any argument other than financial, but at least those who fought against withdrawal of the service kept the trains

provided at one time to carry pedestrians across the cantilever bridge between Connel Ferry and North Connel. Early motorists were also catered for by dint of loading their vehicles onto a flat wagon to be towed across the bridge by the charabanc. What scenes, what character! Now the rails have been ripped up and you drive across the cantilever bridge by car in the blink of an eye, barely registering the experience.

Bare now, except for a bus shelter, the remaining platform at Connel Ferry, together with the neighbouring oil sidings, presents a melancholy scene, and you're only too glad to put it behind you as the train sets off on the last lap to Oban. An overbridge and earthworks to the north of the line are all that remain of a north-west curve never brought into use. The enforced detour inland necessitates some steep climbing - at gradients up to 1 in 50 - to the summit at Glencruitten where there was a loop presided over by a house with a signal box in its front room. The house

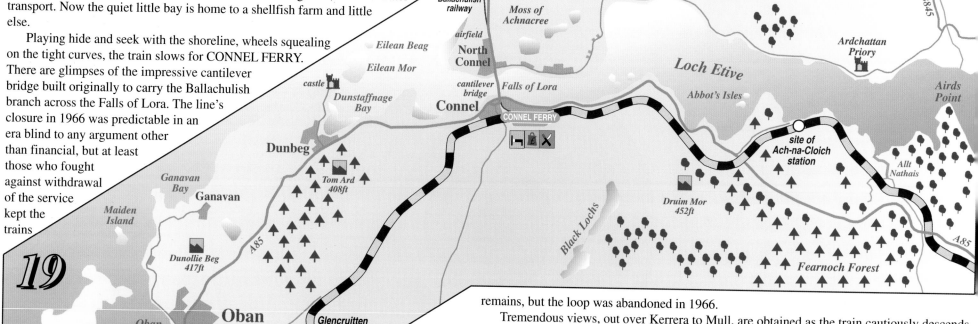

remains, but the loop was abandoned in 1966.

Tremendous views, out over Kerrera to Mull, are obtained as the train cautiously descends into OBAN through rocky cuttings. The gradient is so steep that at times you feel as if you're coming in to land by aeroplane; no wonder most trains leaving Oban in steam days were double-headed as far as Connel. Is it the wheels squealing or the seagulls? It's hard to be sure as the train comes to a halt at the terminus. The thirtieth of June, 1880 was a big day - perhaps the biggest - in the annals of Oban town. Speeches, banquets, bell-ringing and processions marked the railway's opening. A special party of dignitaries representing the shareholding London & North Western Railway sailed into Oban Bay from Liverpool. The C&O had erected a dignified station on the quayside with a large timber-framed trainshed, most regrettably demolished in recent years on safety grounds. Never mind, the railway survives - long may it do so.

going for a couple of extra years. For such a remote railway, it was well-photographed, and delightful pictures of its McIntosh 0-4-4 tanks abound in the railway press. More curiously, a charabanc was

Main picture: One of the most *beautiful* sights on the Oban line - Kilchurn Castle on the banks of Loch Awe.
Inset: One of the most *welcoming* sights on the Oban line - the cafe carriage at Loch Awe.

Dennis Hardley

NRM - Chris Hogg & Lynn Patrick

Cab Ride to MALLAIG

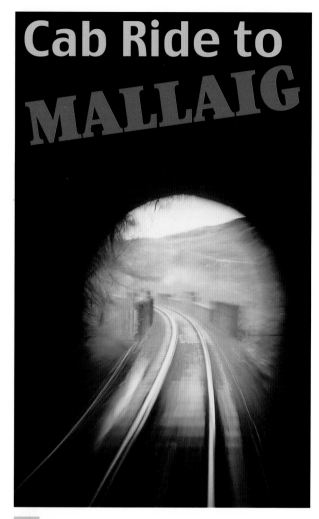

I will gloss over the one-forty a.m. start from Crewe, and the fitful sleeper sleep. Glasgow didn't have its dentures in. Frost on the shoulders of the statues in George Square, and so slippery underfoot that I all but collided with a car coming quickly out of Queen Street. Being, for a scary moment, more likely to end up in the Western Infirmary than Mallaig.

Queen Street is sleek and terrazzo-tiled these days. Forty-seven years ago, when I made my first railway journey - emigrating from Scotland to England aboard the *Queen*

of Scots Pullman - it was a Gothic cavern of smoke and noise and goblins. Pullman service: specially small cutlery for the two year old me, a deferential blind eye to our not quite 'top drawer' collie under the table - all journeys have their fellow passengers in space and time.

On Platform 6 the 08.12 to Mallaig was pawing the track, impatient for departure. Eschewing the sybaritism of the saloon, my place was in the cab with Driver Duncan MacLean and Team Leader Jim Palmer. Back down the train, the guard - 'Big Jim' - busied himself with the passengers. We busied ourselves with the conundrum of fitting three men into a spacially-challenged cab normally occupied by one.

The *Queen of Scots* would have been given a helpful shove out of Queen Street by a banker - Sprinters manage Cowlairs incline on their own account, emerging from the tunnel as dawn opened the curtains over Glasgow's north-eastern suburbs. Forging west through Maryhill, we roared past rimy platforms populated by commuters, waiting to be plucked from their dormitories and thrust into the city centre for another working week.

In the frosty sky a plane descended towards Glasgow Airport. At Singer we passed a shop called 'What Everyone Wants', yet I somehow doubted its ability to fulfil the offer implicit. Blocks of tenements at Dalmuir (featured in Panamint's 'new' 1960 video remake *West Highland*) have been infiltrated by high-rise blocks, creating an uncomfortable feeling of horizontal/vertical dissonance. Duncan's tea mug exposed his passion for 'The Gers'. Proudly he told me he had been 'an Eastfield man'. He had signed-on at five thirty-eight and already been to Stirling and back on an earlier service. Beyond Crianlarich he was to drive the front unit to Oban while Jim and I continued with a fresh driver from Fort William.

Jim hailed from Ardrossan where he'd once worked in a pub. "A man came in one day and said I ought to work for the railway. It seemed like a good idea at the time. I got a job on Ardrossan station, then I became a guard, but I was a poor guard so I trained as a driver."

"Aye, and he was an even poorer driver," broke in Duncan, and I knew that I had finally tuned in to the Scottish dry humour wavelength and that the five and a half hours

spent swaying on the footplate on the iron road to the Western Isles would be accompanied by a good deal of merriment.

Indeed, the *craic* was so good that we were skimming past the Clyde at Bowling before I had time to take stock of my surroundings. The calm, shipless estuary was saffron-tinted, and on the far side a Strathclyde cream and red coloured electric was racing us down to Gourock.

At Helensburgh Upper the mysteries of radio signalling were explained to me. And because I failed O level Science, to a certain extent they remain a mystery. But I can tell you that at every station the driver of West Highland trains contacts control at Banavie and obtains a 'virtual' token which ensures that he has sole occupation of the line ahead, and that as he leaves each station and passes a 'see clear' signboard of blue diagonals on white, he must contact Banavie again and confirm his progress. When this system was introduced in 1988 it rid the West Highland of dozens of signalboxes and signalmen. Progress can be an unpalatable feast, yet the resultant reduction in maintenance and wages may well have swung the balance between us having a railway to Mallaig and us not.

At Garelochhead a menacing-looking man wearing a Partick Thistle scarf and drinking from a can of Irn-Bru alighted from the train - they don't come much tougher than that. We rode beside Loch Long, milky and opaque in the rising morning mist. An elderly couple - our first West Highland passengers, boarded at Arrochar. Loch Lomond looked lovelier than on any other occasion during my field trips and reconnaissance missions. For once I could even see the sharp head of Ben Lomond.

At Ardlui we met the first southbound passenger train of the day, whose Mallaig and Oban portions had been joined at the hip at Crianlarich. Duncan and Jim reminisced as we wound up Glen Falloch. "You knew all the signalmen by sight and you'd often drop groceries off for them," Duncan told me.

"I once had to buy a white rat for a wee girl at Corrour," laughed Jim. "She was one of the Morgans. She asked me if I could get her a rat and a cage next time I was shopping in Glasgow. I brought it back up in the cab with me."

"We carried emergency boxes in the cab," said Duncan. "Smoke canisters and flares in case they had to send out

John Hynds works the point plunger at Crianlarich

have a tendency to wander off into the tea room and not re-emerge until the train has rattled away down Glen Fillan. Apparently the front portion to Oban usually gets away quite quickly and it's not unknown for people left behind to be shoved in a van to chase after the train, especially if it's vital that they make a ferry connection at Oban. You have been warned!

Jim and I bid a quick farewell to Duncan and scurried down the icy platform to the rear unit which had already been uncoupled by Fort William driver John Hynds. With all our passengers safely extracted from George Cull's tea room, John drove the unit up to the end of the platform and got out to operate the point plunger which would route us on to the Fort William line.

John Hynds had driven the early morning train down from Fort William and would work back through to Mallaig. "I was almost playing skittles with the stags this morning," he told us "they come down off the hill to feed at this time of day." John's dad had been a signalman in Dumfriesshire. A railway career was inevitable.

John is one of five ScotRail drivers currently stationed at Fort William. There are another five at Oban and four at Mallaig as well. One of his duties is to drive the Caledonian Sleeper between Fort William and Rannoch, a job he relishes because he gets to rub shoulders with real locomotives as opposed to Sprinters. Privatisation spelt an end to variety for most locomotive crewmen who would, in British Rail days, have worked a number of different types of motive power on both passenger and goods duties, and I sensed that many of the men missed the challenge of handling different types of train. John Hynds had also fired and driven the Fort William-Mallaig steam train in BR days, and regretted its privatisation too.

We paused at Tyndrum to radio through for a fresh token, coming under the jurisdiction of Banavie's North Panel for the first time. Rumbling round the Horseshoe Curve under a sugar-icing-coated Beinn Dorain, I was conscious of my good fortune in being treated to a driver's eye view of the line, something denied to mere passengers since the withdrawal of observation cars.

Beyond Bridge of Orchy the snow lay deeper. John

a search party on the Moor, and Mars bars to keep us going."

"Sometimes you would drive the train across Rannoch," added Jim "and the snow was so deep it obscured the track."

I had a mental image of the train ski-ing over the Moor like a snow-mobile. "We'll see the snow shed after Rannoch," said Jim.

"Snow shed, snow tunnel, 's no' fair." quipped Duncan.

Still giggling, we dropped down into Crianlarich. Duncan and Jim told me that, in spite of refreshment trolleys accompanying most West Highland services, passengers

told us about a stag he'd come upon stuck between the wires of the lineside fence. "We passed it on the way down and stopped to see what we could do on the way back. It was going ballistic. We shouted at it to settle down and, amazingly it did, staying absolutely still as we cut away the wire and then rushing off without even saying thank you. All the passengers applauded when we got back on the train though!"

Every so often we passed a surfaceman's cottage - or, more sadly, their remains - where the platelayer responsible

Driver's eye view of the Horseshoe Curve

for each section of line - together with his family - would have eked out a lonely existence. Jim pointed out one on the climb to Gorton which had found a new lease of life as ScotRail's Walking Club bothy. Some of the long demolished ones continue to grow fresh harvests of perennial flowers, long after their gardens were last attended to.

Rannoch was a Christmas card wilderness, translucent under a cornflower blue sky. John related the legend of Sword Loch, where two clan chieftains had symbolically buried their differences by hurling their swords into the water, and about a ruined house at Lubnaclach which, in steam days, had provided hospitality for passing engine crews who, with mysterious frequency, had found themselves forced to stop for a 'blow-up' in the vicinity.

At Corrour a party of seemingly ill-equipped walkers detrained; one of them, incredibly, hobbling about on crutches. Privately, I figured they'd get no further than the guys in *Trainspotting.* - "Doesn't it make you proud to be Scottish!" John thought we should be able to see Ben Nevis at the next bend in the line, but big lumpy clouds were beginning to bubble up in the west and I had to take his word for it.

Descending by Loch Treig we heard the story of a recluse who lived in a loch-side cabin and made his own, reputedly devastating, beer and wine. Tulloch and Roy Bridge didn't trouble us with passengers, but at Spean Bridge it felt like we were a commuter train, which perhaps we were. "That's Jimmy McNicol," said John, pointing out an elderly man apparently pruning shrubs without the aid of secateurs. "He keeps his gardening tools in the old signalbox." What would the lineside communities do without their railway, I thought, realising, not for the first time, that a railway line acts like an interpreter, making commerce possible between visitors and locals, and indispensable to both.

On the way into Fort William John pointed out the premises of the Railway Social Club of which he is the current Secretary, and I found it comforting to discover that, even post privatisation, the railway community continues to flourish as a brotherhood. Jim left us at Fort William, returning on the noon southbound departure for Glasgow so as to get home at a reasonable hour. John and I swapped cabs and prepared to take the train on to Mallaig.

It's difficult to escape the feeling that the Mallaig Extension is very much an addendum, a sort of supplement to the main line. In fact it supports a slightly more intensive service - well, one more train each way a day. Uncannily, it is quite different in character from the Craigendoran-Fort William section of the West Highland, and even if you are making the through journey from Glasgow, the mere act of reversing out of Fort William station emphasises a new journey about to begin.

In the yard we caught a glimpse of the new turntable, awaiting installation of a corresponding structure at Mallaig before it can fully come into its own. Two radio-fitted, Canadian-built, General Motors Class 66 locomotives were stabled between duties, the EWS Enterprise and Alcan alumina freight services respectively. "There was a Thirty-seven in the yard this morning," John told me, "but that's probably gone round to Corpach with the wagons off the Mossend Enterprise." We rumbled over the Lochy and slowed for Banavie; right under the noses of the radio signalmen.

Trundling along the shore of Loch Eil, John recalled his early footplate career, revealing

a fondness for the Birmingham Railway Carriage & Wagon Class 27 locomotives which hauled most services on the line - passenger and goods alike - until the coming of the Class 37s in the early 1980s. "We used the Twenty-seven's on timber trains from Crianlarich Lower to Corpach Mill - twenty-three fully loaded wagons - we'd just manage to get over some of the summits, doing no more than five miles an hour!"

Though the weather was gloomier than it had been, the waters of Loch Eil were still exceptionally still. From the marshy, western end of the loch we headed into the hills, twisting through forestry plantations towards what represents the climax of the West Highland in many

Rannoch cab views: the viaduct; the snow shed; the moor!

people's eyes, Glenfinnan Viaduct. West Highland expert, John McGregor, had kindly sent a copy of an article in the May 1901 edition of *Railway Magazine* describing the line shortly after it was built. The author's Edwardian enthusiasm had got the better of him: "Commerce shall shake hands with Nature and thus cement a bargain which contributes as much to the profit of the worldly element as to the bringing about of a wider appreciation of all that makes for the pleasure of Eye and Ear." They don't write like that in the *RM* now!

John kindly stopped the train on the viaduct for me to take some photographs. It wasn't that special a dispensation, for apparently the local drivers are in the habit of doing so for the tourists in the summer months, which led us to discuss ways and means to enhance the inherent theatricality of the Mallaig Extension. Unsurprisingly, John felt that ScotRail had too easily surrendered the initiative where tourism was concerned. Perceiving their core business as the provision of day to day travel, they haven't explored the line's true potential. "If this was Switzerland or Austria they'd be making a lot more of the railway. There'd be panoramic carriages and observation cars. There'd be running commentaries and more opportunities for photography." I couldn't help but agree, having argued similarly for such initiatives on the Settle & Carlisle.

Such talk took us past Loch Eilt, perhaps the loveliest of all West Highland associated lochs. Telford's Road to the Isles was rarely out of sight. It was fun ducking and diving through the small tunnels which characterise the Extension's ground-breaking passage through rocky outcrops. I was

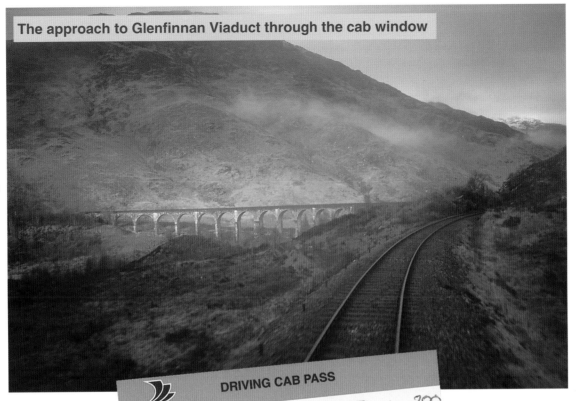

The approach to Glenfinnan Viaduct through the cab window

DRIVING CAB PASS

Pass No : RC20014   Validity : 29 January 200
Name : M. Pearson   Identity Card No : n/9
Dept : —
Valid Routes : Queen St. to Mallaig & return.
Endorsements : n/9
Issued by : Robert Plant
ScotRail Operational Standards Manager

THE HOLDER OF THIS PASS MUST BE ACCOMPANIED

reminded of the Conwy Valley line in North Wales and a relatively recent run I'd had along the line in a 'heritage' diesel multiple unit which offered passengers a view ahead over the driver's shoulder. ScotRail have just got rid of the last of these designs. How well they might have suited the Mallaig Extension; though there would be stiff competition for the front seats.

Dropping down into Arisaig we overtook a coach on the hairpin bends of the neighbouring road. John told me that some Scottish band - the McAlvins I think he said - sing an amusing song about Wallace Arnold coaches on the Road to the Isles. "It's one of the few single track A roads in the country," he said with a shake of his head, "and it can be a bit hair-raising at times." The level crossing at Morar - automated now - gave John the cue to tell me about a driver who'd gained the dubious nickname of 'Sandy the Gatecrasher', not on account of a habit of barging in uninvited on parties, but because he'd once smashed three sets of level crossing gates in a week.

We glided down into Mallaig. I'd been standing up for five fabulously entertaining hours, yet didn't feel remotely tired; running on adrenalin obviously. Five hours as a standing passenger on a busy train might not have been quite so enjoyable. The air on Mallaig station was intoxicating. On the platform we bumped into Arnold Macbeth, a Mallaig driver rostered to take the train back later in the afternoon. John and I strolled across the road to the Fisherman's Mission where, by all accounts, the scones were delicious. In the name of research ...

If there's a moral to this guide book at all, it is that you should not sit slavishly on the train, but that you should get off and explore the often achingly beautiful countryside and coastline it links you to. We are not Egon Ronay, we are not the Scottish Mountaineering Club, all the facilities and suggestions listed in this gazetteer are by way of being ideas for your own personal development; points of departure if you prefer. To the best of our knowledge the entries are accurate at the time of going to press, but we would urge you to use the telephone or the internet to check ahead of your journey for your own peace of mind. Make good use of the local Tourist Information Centres who are unfailingly courteous and models of patience and humour in the face of the most inane tourist enquiry.

ARDLUI
Map 5

With a population numbering barely fifty, Ardlui might be considered lucky still to have a station. A passenger ferry operates across the loch to Ardleish during the summer providing access to the West Highland Way.

Accommodation & Eating Out
ARDLUI HOTEL - Tel: 01301 704243. Two-star country house hotel well-located on the banks of the loch; open all year round.

Shopping
Small general store adjacent to hotel.

Things to Do
Take the ferry (01301 704243) across Loch Lomond.
Boat hire and watersports from LOCH LOMOND WATER PARK - Tel: 01505 382222. Climb (if you're fit and well-prepared!) to the summit of Ben Vorlich.
Walk to Tarbet via Loch Sloy (12 miles) or Crianlarich via Glen Falloch (10 miles).

ARROCHAR
Map 4

Not perhaps the place it was when the steamer pier was still in business, 'Arrowcar' nevertheless remains a useful base camp for those intent on forays into the eponymous Alps. Do note, however, that the village centre lies approximately a mile west of the railway station and the road can be busy.

Accommodation & Eating Out
THE VILLAGE INN - Tel: 01301 702279. Homely pub overlooking Loch Long. Good food and inexpensive accommodation.
LOCH LONG HOTEL - Tel: 01301 702434. Large three star hotel; open February to December. *Also: diner, coffee shop and fish & chips.*

Shopping
Post office, grocery, general store and craft shop.

Things to Do
The ascent of The Cobbler is for serious walkers and climbers, for the less committed delightful woodland walks are available adjacent to the station. Via Glen Loin and Loch Sloy you can walk to the next station up the line, Ardlui, 12 miles away.

ARISAIG
Map 15

Back of beyond village on the shores of Loch nan Ceall - to all intents and purposes the Atlantic Ocean. In the church a clock commemorates the poet Alistair MacDonald. Another literary connection lies in the fact that Arisaig was the birthplace of Long John Silver who went on to work for the lighthouse designer Thomas Stevenson, father of Robert Louis, who was so taken with the lanky Highlander that he immortalised him in *Treasure Island*.

Accommodation & Eating Out
ARISAIG HOTEL - Tel: 01687 450210. Three star waterside hotel. Bar and restaurant meals.
THE OLD LIBRARY LODGE - Tel: 01687 450651. Similarly well sited as above. Taste of Scotland recommended. Open April to October.
Also worth trying - Arisaig Coffee Shop.

Shopping
Spar shop open daily and post office & newsagent. Local crafts from gift shop adjunct to Arisaig Hotel.

Things to Do
LAND SEA & ISLANDS CENTRE - Tel: 01687 450266. Lovely little museum devoted to the interpretation of the locality. Learn about Long John Silver, Bonnie Prince Charlie and the training of secret agents hereabouts during the Second World War.
ARISAIG CRUISES - Tel: 01687 450224. Magical cruises in the summer months to Eigg and Muck and Rhum.

BANAVIE
Map 13

Effectively a suburb of Fort William these days. Alight here for towpath walks along the Caledonian Canal and the Neptune's Staircase lock flight which raises the canal sixty-four feet at this point. Good views of Ben Nevis.

Accommodation & Eating Out
THE MOORINGS HOTEL - Tel: 01397 772797. Comfortable modern four star hotel with Taste of Scotland award winning restaurant.

Things to Do
CALEDONIAN ACTIVITY BREAKS - Tel: 01397 772373. Mountain bike hire - easy access to traffic-free Caledonian Canal towpath.

BEASDALE
Map 15

A bare platform in the woods. Alight here for the exclusive ARISAIG HOUSE 4 star hotel (Tel: 01687 450622) a country house commandeered during the Second World War for the training of the Special Operations Executive. One skill they learnt which will make railway enthusiasts wince, was the blowing-up of locomotives and rolling stock. Apparently the LMS donated some discarded equipment to practise on.

BRIDGE OF ORCHY
Map 8

Not as impressive as it sounds, Bridge of Orchy is a shopless hamlet on the A82 and West Highland Way best known as a popular base camp for would-be ascenders of Beinn Dorain.

Accommodation & Eating Out
BRIDGE OF ORCHY HOTEL - Tel: 01838 400208. Well-appointed four star hotel open all year round. Bar and restaurant meals. Also provides a bunkhouse facility.

Things to Do
Climb to top of Beinn Dorain, a round trip of approximately 6 miles for the stout of footwear and stout of heart. Follow the West Highland Way to Tyndrum - 7 miles.
Linear walks to Rannoch station via either Loch Tulla and Kinghouse (easier-going, 24 miles) or Gorton and Bridge of Gaur (tougher, 25 miles).

CONNEL FERRY
Map 19

Village overlooking the Falls of Lora, a tide race at the mouth of Loch Etive. Worth visiting for a close-up view of the former Ballachulish railway's massive cantilever bridge.

Accommodation & Eating Out
FALLS OF LORA HOTEL - Tel: 01631 710483. Two star Victorian hotel open February to December.
DUNSTAFFNAGE ARMS HOTEL - Tel: 01631 710666. Comfortable one star hotel on A85. Bar meals.
Also: post office stores and Celtic craft shop.

CORPACH
Map 13

Lochside village dominated by huge paper mill. Interesting church with monument and entrance lock to Caledonian Canal.

Accommodation
BUNKSVILLE - Tel: 01397 772467. Bunkhouse and hostel adjacent to station.

Shopping
SPAR and CO-OP.

Things to Do
SNOWGOOSE MOUNTAIN CENTRE - Tel: 01397 772467. Activity centre. Climbing, canoeing, training courses etc.
TREASURES OF THE EARTH - Tel: 01397 772283. Imaginatively displayed collection of gemstones, crystals and fossils. Open daily, gift shop.

CORROUR
Map 10

A wayside halt (pronounced to rhyme with hour) that makes Rannoch look like Clapham Junction. Prior to 1934 the station served only railwaymen and the owners and staff of the Corrour Estate. Bona fide visitors were once taken by private steamer along Loch Ossian to the shooting lodge. The current owners - husband and wife Harvard professors, the Koerners - have ambitious plans for the estate and are rebuilding the shooting lodge on a grand scale.

Accommodation & Eating Out
STATION HOUSE RESTAURANT - Rick & Angela Brown run this well-appointed restaurant and it has the quality of a mirage in a desert, but we can vouch for its authenticity, ambience and comfort. They also sell provisions and souvenirs. We advise you telephone ahead to check opening times on 01397 732236.www.corrour.co.uk
CORROUR BUNKHOUSE - accommodation for up to 14 people in two rooms. Tel: 01397 732236.

continued over

continued:

LOCH OSSIAN YOUTH HOSTEL - 1 mile east of station. Tel: 01397 732207.

Things to Do

Pure, unadulterated walking country. Corrour Estate's web site (www.corrour.co.uk) publishes three entertaining walks in the vicinity: a 9 mile circular walk around Loch Ossian (allow 4 or 5 hours); an out and back walk of 9 miles to Loch Treig; or an 8 mile return ascent of Leum Uilleim, the neighbouring peak, not quite a Munro but a Corbett of 2972ft. For the more fleet of foot and ambitious, Ben Alder looms temptingly over the north-eastern horizon.

George Cull, Crianlarich Station Tearoom

CRIANLARICH   Map 6

Purposeful village strung out along the River Fillan where the A82 and A85 briefly merge. The West Highland Way follows an old military road through conifer plantations half a mile to the west and a Youth Hostel caters for weary backpackers.

Accommodation & Eating Out

STATION TEAROOM - Tel: 01838 300204. Cooked meals, and light snacks. Pre-arranged take-away service (book by 'phone in advance). Gifts and railway souvenirs.
ROD & REEL - Tel: 01838 300271. Lounge bar and restaurant on A85 three minutes walk from the station.
BEN MORE LODGE - Tel: 01838 300210. Three star hotel with bar and restaurant facilities five minutes walk east of station.
YOUTH HOSTEL - Tel: 01838 300260. Adjacent station, closed January.

Shopping

SLAVEN'S post office stores open daily. Tel: 01838 300245.

Things to Do

Local Forestry Commission walks.
Linear walks via West Highland Way to Tyndrum - 7 miles.
Seven mile return trip to the top of Ben More (3843ft) - very steep!

Connections

Buses to Stirling and beyond via Killin. Tel: 01786 44207.
Postbus to Killin - Tel: 01463 256338.

DALMALLY   Map 17

Regular cattle marts disturb the peace of this pleasant village with a long history picturesquely set in the Strath of Orchy. John Smith, former leader of the Labour Party was born here in 1938. Worth alighting from the train and striding out along the old military road for just over a mile to the impressive monument which celebrates the 18th century Gaelic poet Duncan Ban MacIntyre.

Accommodation & Eating Out

GLENORCHY LODGE HOTEL - Tel: 01838 200312. Small two star family run hotel near station.

Shopping

General store, post office and pharmacy.

Things to Do

Local forest walks, monument walk (see above), and linear walk to Tyndrum (12 miles).

FALLS OF CRUACHAN Map 18

CRUACHAN POWER STATION VISITOR CENTRE - Tel: 01866 822618. Guided tours inside the 'hollow mountain' by electric bus - see the massive generators, learn about hydro-electricity, return to the cafeteria and gift shop. Open daily Easter to November.

FORT WILLIAM   Maps 12 & 13

It continues to rankle diehards that the name Fort William celebrates King William of Orange, no lover of the Highlanders - imagine how the Sassenachs would feel if the Forty-five had been successful and London was forever after known as Charlieville. Old wounds apart, 'The Fort' is a thriving commercial and tourist centre atmospherically located between Ben Nevis and Loch Linnhe. A stroll down the High Street should be enough to convince you that 'your heart's in the Highlands'.

Accommodation & Eating Out

ALEXANDRA HOTEL - The Parade. Tel: 01397 702241. Traditional two star hotel adjacent to railway station and town centre.
MILTON HOTEL - North Road. Tel: 01397 702331. Modern two star hotel with leisure club, open all year round.
FORT WILLIAM BACKPACKERS - Alam Road. Tel: 01397 700711.
TRAVEL INN - Tel: 01397 703707. Adjacent station.
LOCH IALL - Brewers Fayre restaurant adjunct to above.
LOCHABER SIDING - station buffet with a difference, local produce and crafts.
CRANNOG RESTAURANT - Town Pier. Tel: 01397 705589. Beautifully located fish restaurant.
McTAVISH'S KITCHEN - High Street. Tel: 01397 702406. Scottish food and Scottish dancing.
GROG & GRUEL - High Street. Tel: 01397 705078. CAMRA recommended ale house and restaurant.
NICO'S - High Street. Tel: 01397 700121. Eat in or takeaway fish & chips.
NEVISPORT - Airds Crossing. Tel: 01397 700707. Restaurant bar and coffee shop - big breakfasts for famished guide researchers. See also under Shopping.
McDONALDS - eat in/takeaway hamburgers adjacent to station.

Shopping

NEVISPORT (two minutes walk through the subway from the station) is a good port of call for stocking up on West Highland guide books and maps. Outdoor clothing and gift departments as well. Tel: 01397 704921. Further along the Hiigh Street you'll discover that many retailers cling on to the old traditions of personal service and friendliness, no better example being MACLENNAN & Co on the High Street, kilt outfitters since 1860, and now owners of an excellent delicatessen too.

Things to Do

TOURIST INFORMATION - Cameron Square. Tel: 01397 703781.
SEAL ISLAND CRUISES - ninety minute trips on Loch Linnhe; great views of Ben Nevis when it isn't in the clouds! Tel: 0374 207135.
BEN NEVIS DISTILLERY - Visitor Centre and distillery tours. Tel: 01397 700200.
THE WEST HIGHLAND MUSEUM - Cameron Square. Local history vividly displayed. Tel: 01397 702169.

Connections

OFF BEAT BIKES - 117 High Street. Tel: 01397 704008. Bicycle hire.
MOTORWAY CARS - Ford Rental cars located at An Aird adjacent to the railway station. Special discounts for ScotRail Caledonian Sleeper ticket holders. Tel: 01397 702030.
AL'S TAXIS - Tel: 01397 702545.
BUSES - Tel: 01463 222244 or 01397 702373 for details of local services.

GARELOCHHEAD   Map 3

Lochside village dominated by the Clyde Naval Base. General store, pizza restaurant, inn and tearoom.

GLENFINNAN   Map 14

Glenfinnan's peerless setting at the head of Loch Shiel contributes to its popularity as a stopover point whether you're on the road or the railway to the isles. Here, in the late afternoon of 19th August 1745, some twelve hundred loyal clansmen raised the standard of Prince Charles Edward Stuart, effectively declaring war on the British throne, and something of the gravitas of that occasion seems still redolent in the craggy landscape. Outside the church stands an unusual bell in its own framework. Apparently it was cast too heavy to hang in the belfry and has stood outside ever since.

Accommodation & Eating Out

GLENFINNAN STATION - railway dining car and sleeping carriage. John Barnes and his Norwegian wife Hege run these two distinctive railway vehicles (Mk1 Standards for the cognoscenti) in addition to the Station Museum. The sleeping car can be hired exclusively by groups or also functions as a slightly offbeat bunkhouse. Tel: 01397 722295.
THE PRINCE'S HOUSE - Tel: 01397 722246. Comfortable Les Routiers recommended three star hotel (open March to November) close to the railway station. Flora's restaurant open to non residents.
GLENFINNAN HOUSE HOTEL - Tel: 01397 722235. Lochside two star hotel run on traditional lines. Open April to October.

Things to Do

GLENFINNAN STATION MUSEUM - Tel: 01397 722295. Cosy little shrine to West Highland matters created by railway enthusiast John Barnes. Small shop selling souvenirs.

GLENFINNAN MONUMENT & VISITOR CENTRE - Tel: 01397 722250. National Trust for Scotland interpretive centre located on A830 about ten minutes walk from the station. LOCH SHIEL CRUISES - Tel: 01397 722235. Cruises of varying length and destination in the wake of Bonnie Prince Charlie aboard the ex-admiralty launch *Sileas*.

HELENSBURGH   *Map 2*

Gateway to the West Highland railway, this Victorian characterful resort and dormitory was created (and named after his wife) by Sir James Colquhorn in 1776. Other luminaries include Henry Bell, designer of the first commercially successful steam ship; the former Prime Minister, Andrew Bonar Law; and John Logie Baird, inventor of the television. A passenger ferry operates across the Clyde to Gourock via Kilcreggan.

Eating Out

HUMBLES - Colquhoun Square. Italian cafe bar frequented by the cream of Helensburgh society. Tel: 01436 674500.

Shopping

Enjoyable place to shop, with many 'good old fashioned' Scots retailers in evidence - like SOMERVILLE or CALLAGHAN the butchers and COYLE the fishmongers on West Princes Street. Railway modellers will be tempted into MAC'S Model Railroading shop on Sinclair Street which cleverly also deals in doll's houses! McLARENS secondhand bookshop on Clyde Street (west end of seafront opp bust of Logie Baird) has a particularly excellent stock of nautical and maritime titles.

Things to Do

TOURIST INFORMATION - The Clock Tower, The Pier. Tel: 01436 672642. Open April to October only.
THE HILL HOUSE - 5 minutes walk to north of 'Upper' station, the celebrated Scots architect and artist Charles Rennie Mackintosh designed this wonderful house for the publisher Walter Blackie in 1902. It should be a 'must' in any itinerary purporting to cover the West Highland railway. Open daily April to October under the aegis of the National Trust for Scotland. Tel: 01436 673900. Also available for holiday lets via the Landmark Trust - Tel: 01628 825925.

LOCHAILORT   *Map 15*

Isolated request halt at the head of an eponymous sea loch. A nearby lineside monument remembers Susan McCallum, landlady of the local inn for seventeen years prior to her death in 1890. Inverailort Castle was the scene of Commando and SoE training during the Second World War; Peter Churchill and Odette were put through their respective paces here. More recently it was used as a film set for a Harry Potter film!

Accommodation & Eating Out

LOCHAILORT INN - Tel: 01687 470208. Cosy two star hotel. Bar meals.

LOCH AWE   *Map 18*

Idyllic lochside community created with the coming of the railway. On the waterfront there's a memorial to Robert the Bruce who won a decisive battle nearby in 1308. Sprinkled around the loch are crannogs - artifical islands dating from the Bronze Age.

Accommodation & Eating Out

LOCH AWE HOTEL - Tel: 01838 200261. Large three star hotel overlooking loch, open February to December.
TIGHT LINE - Tel: 01838 200215. Bar on A85.
LOCHSIDE CAFE - housed in former railway carriage adjacent to station.

Shopping

LOCH AWE STORES - Tel: 01838 200200. Open daily: food, gifts, newspapers, post office and fishing permits.

Things to Do

LOCH AWE STEAM PACKET - Tel: 01866 833333 or 200440. Loch cruises and ferry across to Kilchurn Castle from the pier by the railway station; April to November.
KILCHURN CASTLE - 15th century keep struck by lightning in 1769 and subsequently a picturesque ruin. Ferry from pier or 3 mile return walk round via road.
ST CONAN'S KIRK - small jewel of a Victorian church on A85, fifteen minutes walk west of station.

LOCH EIL O.B.   *Map 13*

Station for adjacent Outward Bound Centre. Tel: 01397 772866.

LOCHEILSIDE   *Map 13*

Idyllic lochside platform lacking any visible means of support.

Mallaig Harbour

MALLAIG   *Map 16*

The end of the line in one sense, the beginning of things in another, Mallaig resembles some remote seaboard town in Norway or Iceland and simply oozes with atmosphere. Apart from tourism, fishing is still Mallaig's primary commercial activity, though from time to time the threat of oil rears its ugly head. Prawns are the main catch nowadays, from fishing grounds out by Canna and Eigg and Rhum. Mallaig Kippers may still be flaunted as a local delicacy, but in the modern world of global fishmarkets, more likely than not these will have been caught in Canada and simply *smoked* in Mallaig. By the same token much of Mallaig's fish harvest is taken away (not, alas, by rail anymore) for processing as far away as Grimsby.

Accommodation & Eating Out

MARINE HOTEL - Tel: 01687 462217. Three star family run hotel on harbour's edge. 'Taste of Scotland' bar meals.
WEST HIGHLAND HOTEL - Tel: 01687 462210. Two star family run hotel, open March to October. Bar lunches for non residents.
SHEENA'S BACKPACKERS LODGE - Tel: 01687 462764. Bunkhouse.
FISHERMENS MISSION - Tel: 01687 462086. Homely cafeteria where you can eavesdrop on the local gossip. Shower facilities.
THE FISH MARKET - Tel: 01687 462299. Comfortable restaurant with harbour views.

THE CABIN SEAFOOD RESTAURANT - Tel: 01687 462207. Fish teas, shellfish and massive lobster platters. Also fish & chip takeaways best partaken on the harbour wall with the seals for company.
Several other places to eat - bars, cafes, restaurants.

Shopping

Plenty of interest to keep the female of the species content between trains. Fresh fish from the long established JAFFY'S (Tel: 01687 462224) or ANDY RACE (Tel: 01687 462626); gifts from THE BOAT HOUSE (Tel: 01687 462604) ; provisions from SPAR POST OFFICE or NEVIS STORES. *Also: chemist, bookshop, clothes and toys.*

Things to Do

TOURIST INFORMATION - Tel: 01687 462170.
HERITAGE CENTRE - Tel: 01687 462085. Local history displays including a good deal about the railway.
MARINE WORLD - Tel: 01687 462292.
CALEDONIAN MacBRAYNE - sailings to Armadale (Skye) and the Small Isles (Eigg, Muck, Canna and Rhum). Tel: 01687 462403.
BRUCE WATT SEA CRUISES - morning, afternoon or whole day cruises on Loch Nevis for stunning scenery and chance encounters with whales, seals and dolphins. Tel: 01687 462320.
MINCH CHARTERS - twice daily mini cruises, charters etc. Tel: 01687 462304.
There are several short coastal and/or hill walks to be enjoyed in the vicinity but you sense you should be afloat to do Mallaig and its setting justice.

MORAR   *Map 16*

Famed for its white or silver sands and splendid views of Eigg and Rhum, Morar is an incredibly romantic spot at which to leave the train. Inland, the deepest loch in Scotland waits to be explored, whilst out towards the islands, Tir nan Og, the Gaelic paradise, seems almost tangible. *Note that there are no facilities other than the hotel.*

Accommodation & Eating Out

MORAR HOTEL - Tel: 01687 462346. Two star family run hotel where Bax composed. Open April to October; bar and restaurant meals.

OBAN

Map 19

The travel writer Paul Theroux called Oban: "a dull clean town on a coast of wild water and islands." Given the context of its isolated setting this 'dull' town seems positively metropolitan. With a population of eight thousand it is second only to Fort William in the West Highlands. Added to which its status as a resort and port for the Western Isles lends it a gravitas and feeling of activity that rail travellers would be forgiven for thinking they had left behind in Glasgow. Though its history goes back earlier, Oban's impetus came from the arrival of the railway and its development as a port, and behind the frivolity of its holidaymaking crowds, the everyday life of the locals goes on with an admirable sense of self-sufficiency. As all the postcards depict, the town is crowned by McCaig's Tower, a massive circular folly built at the instigation of John Stewart McCaig in a philanthropic attempt to salve a period of unemployment amongst the local stone masons. Thankfully, twenty-first century Oban would seem well able to do without such overt demonstrations of charity.

Accommodation & Eating Out
YOUTH HOSTEL - Corran Esplanade. Tel: 01631 562025.
CALEDONIAN HOTEL - Station Square. Large two star hotel within easy reach of the station. Tel: 01631 563133.
BALMORAL HOTEL - Craigard Road. Tel: 01631 562731. Cosy, family run two star hotel with well regarded restaurant open to non-residents.
WATERFRONT RESTAURANT - adjacent railway station. Tel: 01631 563110. Excellent fish restaurant overlooking harbour.
McTAVISH'S KITCHEN - George Street. Tel: 01631 563064. All singing, all dancing Scottish restaurant.
CAFE 41 - Combie Street. Tel: 01631 564117. "Oban's Continental Bistro."
Obviously there are many, many other establishments offering accommodation and refreshment within easy reach of Oban station, not least the local seafood outlets on the adjoining pier.

Things to Do
TOURIST INFORMATION - Argyll Square. Tel: 01631 563122.
It would be remiss of you indeed not to extend your itinerary beyond Oban and set foot on at least one or two of the isles:

Seafood stall, Oban Harbour

CALEDONIAN MacBRAYNE - Tel: 01631 566688. Ferries to Mull, Lismore, Colonsay, Coll, Tiree etc.
GORDON GRANT TOURS - Tel: 01631 562842. Excursions to Mull, Iona, Staffa etc.

Shopping
Plenty of shops in Oban for those in withdrawal or denial. CHALMERS on George Street specialises in Highland Dress. TASTE OF ARGYLL on Stevenson Street is an outlet for local foodstuffs. Last minute gifts can be grabbed from McCAIG'S WAREHOUSE or CAITHNESS GLASS in the Waterfront Centre before you catch the train.

Transport Connections
FLIT car hire - Tel: 01631 566553.

RANNOCH

Map 9

Archetypal wilderness station set in a stony sea of boulders, bog, heather and deer. The railway built the coach road to Kinnloch Rannoch as a means of contact with the outside world. Read R.L.Stevenson's *Kidnapped* to gain a sense of local colour.

Accommodation & Eating Out
MOOR OF RANNOCH HOTEL - Tel: 01882 633238. Exceptionally comfortable small hotel within yards of the station. Beautiful decor reflecting the nature of the district. Restaurant and bar food. Adjoining craft shop selling Highland made gifts.
RENTON COTTAGE - self catering in former railwayman's cottage adjacent to the station. Tel: 0131 225 4906.
STATION TEA ROOM - Tel: 01882 633209. Up for sale as we went to press. It is to be hoped that the new owners carry on the tradition of providing sustenance for all-comers.

Things to Do
Catch the post bus, which (Mon-Sat) meets the morning train from Glasgow, to Pitlochry; two bumpy hours, but a lot of good *craic* away. Tel: 0845 3011130.
Take a fairly strenuous eleven mile walk along the *Road to the Isles* to Corrour, the next station up the line; stroll along the banks of Loch Laidon; or simply soak up the silence between trains.

ROY BRIDGE

Map 11

Nearest station for exploring Monessie Gorge and Glen Roy.
STRONLOSSIT HOTEL - Tel: 01397 712253. Three star hotel adjacent to the railway station. Bar and restaurant meals.
Small Post Office store half a mile from station.

SPEAN BRIDGE

Map 12

Busy village at junction of main roads. Bridge spanning the river originally built by Thomas Telford as part of his road improvement schemes in the early 1800s.

Accommodation & Eating Out
SPEAN BRIDGE HOTEL - Tel: 01397 712250. Two star hotel near station. Contains small museum devoted to the Commandos.
OLD PINES - Tel: 01397 712324. Award-winning restaurant also offering accommodation.
OLD STATION RESTAURANT - Tel: 01397 712535. Restaurant housed in former station building.
LITTLE CHEF - semi-fast food on the A82.

Shopping
Post office and Mace food store.
SPEAN BRIDGE WOOLLEN MILL - Tel: 01397 712260. Weaving demonstrations and Clan tartans. Knitwear, foods & wines, whisky and souvenirs. Coffee Shop.
TOURIST INFORMATION - Tel: 01397 712576. Open Easter to October only.

Things to Do
Pay homage to the Commando Memorial - a mile north-west of the station on the A82. Linear walks to Roy Bridge via Monessie Gorge (8 miles) and Fort William (12 miles).

TARBET

Map 4

Small village on the side of Loch Lomond which shares its station (1 mile west) with Arrochar

Eating Out & Shopping
BLACK SHEEP CRAFTS - adjacent station. Tel: 01301 702364. Crafts and cafe. *Tea room and post office.*

Things to Do
CRUISE LOCH LOMOND - Tarbet Pier. Tel: 01301 702356. Excursions on Loch Lomond. Sail to Inversnaid for lunch and a visit to Rob Roy's Cave.
TOURIST INFORMATION - Main Street. Tel: 01301 702260. Open April to October.

TAYNUILT

Map 18

Lots of scope for excursions and days out from this village scattered about the southern shore of Loch Etive. Facilities in the village centre include: post office, butcher's shop, general store, sweet shop and antiques.

Accommodation & Eating Out
TAYNUILT HOTEL - Tel: 01866 822437. Old coaching inn on A85, less than five minutes walk from station.
POLFEARN HOTEL - Tel: 01866 822251. One star country house hotel overlooking Airds Bay.
ROBIN'S NEST - Tel: 01866 822429. Pleasant tearoom adjacent to station.

Things to Do
LOCH ETIVE CRUISES - Tel: 01866 822430. Three hour trips around the loch.
BONAWE FURNACE - Tel: 01866 822432. Fascinating 18th century iron furnace founded by Cumbrian ironmasters.
INVERAWE - Tel: 01866 822446. Smokery and fisheries, shop, tearoom and nature trails. Open daily March to December.

TULLOCH

Map 11

Tulloch station was originally known as Inverlair, which made more sense, because there is a small settlement there, on the south bank of the Spean, whilst Tulloch, on the north bank, is truly out in the wilds, down a side road off the A86, surrounded by conifer plantations. Rudolph Hess is reputed to have been held prisoner at Inverlair Lodge after his ill-fated solo landing in Renfrewshire and attempt to sue for peace in 1941. Adjacent to Tulloch station building, a military mountain training centre occupies former stables once occupied by the horses which hauled the coaches to Kingussie.

continued over

continued :

Accommodation & Eating Out
STATION LODGE - bunk house beautifully converted from the original Swiss chalet style station building of 1894. Accommodation, dining room, shop, telephone & laundry. Charming hosts - Alan Renwick and Belinda Melville.Ten Munros within *easy* reach! Tel: 01397 732333. www.stationlodge.co.uk

Breakfast at Station Lodge

NRM - Chris Hogg & Lynn Patrick

TYNDRUM
Map 7

A popular coach-stop at the bifurcation of the Oban and Fort William roads. Suspend belief and you could be in Vermont.

Accommodation & Eating Out
INVERVEY HOTEL - Tel: 01838 400219. Two star hotel with bar and restaurant meals.
WEST HIGHLANDER - Tel: 01838 400243. Bunkhouse, diner and mountain bike hire.
STRATHFILLAN WIGWAMS - characterful and inexpensive accommodation hard by the line on Auchtertye Farm two miles south-east of Tyndrum. Tel: 01838 400251.
CLIFTON COFFEE HOUSE - Tel: 01838 400271. Inexpensive eatery adjunct to large gift shop.
LITTLE CHEF - all-day restaurant on A82.

Shopping
GREEN WELLY SHOP - Tel: 01838 400271. Wellingtons, woollies and waterproofs!
G.A.BRODIE - nothing's too much trouble for the friendly owners of this well-stocked general store, off licence and post office established as long ago as 1930. Tel: 01838 400275.

Things to Do
TOURIST INFORMATION - Tel: 01838 400246. Open daily April to October, weekends only in Winter. Staging post on West Highland Way - linear walks to Crianlarich and Bridge of Orchy.

INFORMATION

USING THIS GUIDE
Nineteen, north facing, one inch to one mile maps portray the routes of the West Highland Lines between Glasgow Queen Street, Fort William, Mallaig and Oban. Each map is accompanied by a running commentary on matters historical, topographical and related to railway operation. Emphasis is given to the northward journey in each case, but the details are equally relevant for travel in the opposite direction.

Towards the rear of the guide a gazetteer gives details of all the stations served beyond Helensburgh where the West Highland Lines are usually deemed to commence. This gazetteer gives a brief summary of each place together with itemised information on places to eat and find accommodation, shopping facilities, visitor centres, things to do and useful contacts such as bus links, taxi services and tourist information centres. Where accuracy is essential to the planning of an itinerary you are urged to make contact by telephone to ensure you have up to the minute details.

SCHEDULED SERVICES
Day to day services on the West Highland Lines are operated by ScotRail. Currently there are three trains a day in each direction between Glasgow and Fort William and Glasgow and Oban, with four trains each way per day linking Fort William and Mallaig. Additionally there are sleeper and steam services as detailed below. The average journey time between Glasgow and Fort William is just under four hours; Fort William to Mallaig takes around an hour and a half; Glasgow to Oban takes around three hours. Services are currently provided by comfortable Class 156 'Sprinter' units which provide standard class, non-smoking facilities only. Well stocked catering trolley services are available on the majority of services. Certain services divide at Crianlarich in the northbound direction, usually with the Oban portion leading. A limited number of bicycles can be carried on ScotRail services - see opposite.

SLEEPER TRAINS
The Caledonian Sleeper runs nightly (Saturday excepted) between London Euston and Fort William via Edinburgh (and vice versa) and calls at all the West Highland stations en route. Very comfortable single and twin berth sleeper cabins are obtainable as well as a certain amount of ordinary seating between Edinburgh and Fort William. A Lounge Car accompanies each train offering meals, snacks and drinks. **Telephone 08457 550033 for further details.**

STEAM TRAINS
The Jacobite - a nostalgic steam-hauled train - operates a daily (Saturdays excepted) six hour return trip (including a two hour lunch break at Mallaig) in the summer months between Fort William and Mallaig. Operated by the West Coast Railway Company, reservations are extremely advisable for this popular service, though tickets may be available on the day from Fort William station or the guard on the train. Please note: only West Coast Railway Co tickets are valid on *The Jacobite*. **Tel: 01463 239026 or 01524 732100.**

CHARTER TRAINS
A number of companies run charter trains and excursions over the West Highland Lines. Often these will originate from other parts of the country and offer little or no opportunity for local travel. A recent exception to this, however, has been the Highland Railway Heritage series of steam excursions which have featured tours over the West Highland Lines. **For further details telephone: 01397 722295.** Other regular operators of diesel-hauled excursions over the West Highland Lines include:
The Royal Scotsman - Tel: 0131 555 1344.
Pathfinder Tours - Tel: 01453 835414.
Hertfordshire Rail Tours - Tel: 01438 812125.
Fragonset - Tel: 01827 712689.

TICKETS & TRAVELPASSES
There are ScotRail booking offices at Glasgow Queen Street, Fort William, Mallaig and Oban; all other West Highland Lines stations are unstaffed. A range of tickets is available from these offices and from the guards on board the trains. 50% discounts are available to holders of Highland Railcards. For an idea of fares (including current offers, Travelpasses etc) telephone **National Rail Enquiries on 08457 484950** or visit **ScotRail's website at www.scotrail.co.uk** Tickets in advance are obtainable from **ScotRail Telesales & Bookings. Tel: 08457 550033.**

HOLIDAYS
Fully inclusive Short Breaks, Self-Catering (in Fort William) and Escorted Holidays featuring the West Highland Lines are organised by ScotRail - Tel: 0870 161 0 161.

BICYCLES
Bicycles are conveyed free of charge on ScotRail service trains. The Class 156 'Sprinter' units which provide most of the timetabled services over the West Highland Lines can convey up to six bicycles per 2 car unit. Reservations are *compulsory* and should be made at principal staffed stations or ScotRail Telesales on 08457 550033 up to eight weeks in advance (12 weeks for the Caledonian sleeper service) but no later than two hours before the train *commences* its journey.

READING & VIEWING
The West Highland Railway by John Thomas ISBN 1 899863 07 9
The Callander & ObanRailway by John Thomas ISBN 0 946537 615
Walks from the West Highland Railway by Chris & John Harvey ISBN 1 85284 169 9
West Highland by John Gray BBC/Panamint Cinema (Tel: 01506 834936)
Classic Train Journeys of Scotland by Video 125 (Tel: 01344 628565)

USEFUL CONTACTS
Friends of the West Highland Lines - Tel: 0141 885 0069.

Our Sponsors

Wayzgoose is extremely grateful to the following organisations who have sponsored and encouraged the publication of this guide.

HIGHLAND RAIL PARTNERSHIP

The Highland Rail Partnership is an association of Highland Council, Perth & Kinross Council, Argyll & Bute Council, ScotRail, Railtrack, EWS, Freightliner, Argyll and the Isles Enterprise, Lochaber Limited, Inverness & Nairn Enterprise, Ross & Cromarty Enterprise, Caithness & Sutherland Enterprise, Moray Badenoch & Strathspey Enterprise and the Friends of the Kyle, Far North and West Highland Lines. The Partnership aims to assist the development of passenger, freight and heritage rail business across the Highland area.

ScotRail is Scotland's national passenger train operator, providing over 95% of services north of the border. We run four types of service - suburban round Glasgow and Edinburgh, interurban linking the five Scottish cities, rural in the West and North Highlands and South-West Scotland, and the Caledonian Sleepers which link Fort William, Inverness, Aberdeen, Glasgow and Edinburgh with London. The suburban network supported by Strathclyde Passenger Transport is the largest in Britain outside London, and includes a daily commuter service from Garelochhead. We have refurbished the trains used on the West Highland Lines, and in conjunction with the Scottish Cycle Challenge Fund have doubled the capacity on daytime trains for cycles. Our Highland Railcard offers a 50% discount on fares for local residents, and our Freedom of Scotland Travelpass and Highland Rover tickets include Caledonian MacBrayne ferries and Scottish Citylink routes linking Oban, Campbeltown, Fort William and Inverness. ScotRail Shortbreaks are unaccompanied and escorted holidays which in the West Highlands

are in hotel, self-catering or bunkhouse accommodation. We operate all stations on the West Highland Lines and are keen to build on recent successes in finding new uses for vacant premises.

SPT is Scotland's only passenger transport authority and executive, investing in rail, bus, underground and ferry services for 42% of the nation's population. We finance ScotRail passenger services in the west of Scotland and set train fares and timetables. After more than £400 million of investment over 26 years, we now have the biggest passenger rail network in the UK outside London. Current rail patronage in Strathclyde is 43 million a year - the highest level since 1982. We run the Glasgow Underground and the Renfrew-Yoker ferry. SPT currently subsidises about 150 bus services in areas where local communities are not already served by commercial operators. Our dial-a-Bus service offers accessible transport to people with mobility problems, providing more than 300,000 journeys a year. Information on all our services, products and tickets is available at SPT's expanding network of travel information centres. To find out more about SPT and how we're shaping a future for public transport write to or call us at: Strathclyde Passenger Transport, Consort House, 12 West George Street, Glasgow G2 1HN. Tel: 0141 332 6811.

Highlands & Islands
ENTERPRISE

The Highlands and Islands is a vast and diverse area stretching some 420 miles north to south. The task of the Highlands & Islands Enterprise Network (HIE) is to help create a strong, diverse and sustainable economy where quality of life is matched by quality of opportunity.

The Network has substantial powers and resources to aid economic and social development. It can finance businesses, provide factories and offices, develop and implement training programmes, assist community and cultural projects and undertake environmental

renewal. Assistance and advice is delivered mainly through ten Local Enterprise Companies (LECs) based in the areas they serve. Efficient, accessible and environmentally sustainable transport is vital for the functioning of the economy. The HIE network, in conjunction with local authorities, the rail industry and others is, therefore, a major funder of the Highland Rail Partnership whose aim is to promote rail development in the area.

EWS

EWS - English Welsh & Scottish Railway - is Britain's largest rail freight operator providing a key service for British industry. Daily train services link all parts of Britain with the rest of the country and Europe, and the West Highland Line is a key component of the EWS network. EWS have invested over £700 million in 280 new locomotives and 2,500 new wagons, and the new Class 66 locomotive has been cleared for working on the major part of the West Highland Line. Nearly 1,100 train services are operated a day by EWS, moving over 100 million tonnes a year in markets as diverse as coal, timber, cars and steel. On the West Highland Lines EWS moves timber, paper, china clay and alumina and is continually seeking new traffic flows.

Railtrack in Scotland aims to work with its partners to give Scottish rail passengers and freight users more trains, in shorter journey times and a better overall experience of using the railway network.

Railtrack in Scotland is planning to spend £2.3 billion on the railway network in Scotland over the next ten years. This massive investment will help us to improve facilities and services at our stations to enable all passengers to better enjoy travelling by rail. It is our intention that railway stations will become important transport hubs within local communities, and that much of the decay of

our national railway infrastructure will be redressed, paying heed to our heritage, social and environmental responsibilities. Safety is our number one priority and we have begun a major programme of work installing the Train Protection Warning System on routes across the Scottish network.

As a leading player in the Scottish business community, Railtrack in Scotland takes its social and environmental responsibilities seriously and works with many groups and organisations in an effort to further build partnership links with local communities and lineside neighbours.

Alcan are one of the world's major producers of aluminium, the most versatile of metals. Aluminium's lightness, strength, resistance to corrosion, and attractive appearance make it a natural choice for applications ranging from aircraft to commercial vehicles, packaging to window frames. Even after the useful life of such items is over, aluminium has more to offer - recyclability. Our smelter at Fort William draws water power from a large tract of mountains and glens in the West Highlands, and produces some 40,000 tonnes of aluminium each year We rely on the West Highland Railway for transport, both of incoming raw materials and the delivery of cast ingots. We have been an important employer in Lochaber since the 19th century, and in the future we shall continue to play our part in sustaining the environment and the industrial vigour of the Highlands.

Freightliner's Scottish business is centred on its terminal at Coatbridge from where it operates intermodal services to Fort William. Freightliner Coatbridge is Scotland's largest intermodal facility and it moves the equivalent of 2.7 million tonnes of cargo from Scotland by rail on its Anglo-Scottish services.

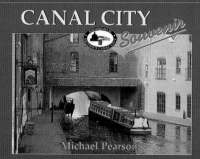